Scrapbooking, Time Capsules, Life Story
Desktop Videography & Beyond with
Poser 5, CorelDRAW ® Graphics Suite 12
& Corel WordPerfect Office Suite 12

# Scrapbooking, Time Capsules, Life Story Desktop Videography & Beyond with Poser 5, CorelDRAW ® Graphics Suite 12 & Corel WordPerfect Office Suite 12

## Use Desktop Publishing and Graphic Design Software to produce Keepsake Albums, Life Stories, and Personal History Time Capsules.

Poser 5 is a 3-Dimensional character and animation design software program that lets you take a photo of yourself or a loved on and animate it on a figure that you can design or use from the software samples, even grow real hair, fur, or grass, and put your loved one in a new or exotic environment for a time capsule of personal history, for example. WordPerfect is perfectly compatible with Microsoft Word documents. You can work back and forth. And Word Perfect has the ability to mimic the interface and keyboard shortcuts of Microsoft Office's main programs—Word, Excel, and PowerPoint. So go ahead and desktop publish those time capsules, life stories, personal histories, scrapbooks or keepsake albums using CorelDRAW ® Graphics Suite 12 & Corel WordPerfect Office Suite 12 and beyond. Here's how to start your business desktop publishing and graphic designing other people's keepsake albums and time capsules using Poser 5 and Corel's graphics and office suites to be a personal historian in print, on video, and on DVD, CD, and the Web. This book is about what questions to ask rather than about the software and video techniques. It's about the big picture strategies of what to put on that DVD, CD, tape, or multimedia Web presentation and how to gather the information rather than about how to manipulate the software. This time capsule beyond scrapbooking guide shows you the big picture on how to gather the information and what questions to ask. For software techniques, go to the Web sites of the software manufacturers. They have expert trainers and training materials in the use and application of the software. Here's the content of what to put on the software.

*Presented by Anne Hart*

ASJA Press

New York  Lincoln  Shanghai

Scrapbooking, Time Capsules, Life Story Desktop Videography &
Beyond with Poser 5, CorelDRAW ® Graphics Suite 12 & Corel
WordPerfect Office Suite 12
Use Desktop Publishing and Graphic Design Software to produce Keepsake
Albums, Life Stories, and Personal History Time Capsules.

ASJA Press
an imprint of iUniverse, Inc.

For information address:
iUniverse, Inc.
2021 Pine Lake Road, Suite 100
Lincoln, NE 68512
www.iuniverse.com

ISBN: 0-595-33227-7

Printed in the United States of America

# Introduction

How to use Poser 5 and Corel Graphics Suite and Corel WordPerfect to Be a Scrap Booker (Keepsake Album Crafter), Personal Historian, Time Capsule Maker, Videographer, Genealogist, Writer, Desktop Publisher, Graphic Designer, or Documentarian.

1. Put Direct Experience In A Small Package And Launch It Worldwide.

2. Write, Record, & Publish Purpose-Driven Personal History
Dramatize, Package, Promote, Present, & Launch Your Purpose

3. Edit, Dramatize, Package, Promote, Present, Publish, Record, Produce, & Launch Time Capsules of Personal Histories, Autobiographies, Biographies, Vignettes, and Eulogies and/or DNA-Driven Genealogy Reports: Launching the Inspiration-Driven or Design-Driven Life Story and Detailing Your Purpose.

# TABLE OF CONTENTS LINKS

1. Put Direct Experience In A Small Package And Launch It Worldwide.

2. Write, Record, & Publish Purpose-Driven Personal History
Dramatize, Package, Promote, Present, & Launch Your Purpose

3. Edit, Dramatize, Package, Promote, Present, Publish, Record, Produce, & Launch Time Capsules of Personal Histories, Autobiographies, Biographies, Vignettes, and Eulogies: Launching the Inspiration-Driven or Design-Driven Life Story and Detailing Your Purpose.

Use Simplicity and Commitment in Personal History Writing, Time Capsules, and Videos.

Here's useful insight to those who may someday write fiction, or their life stories, true experiences, or other people's life stories as vignettes or books created by linking a dozen or more vignettes together into a publishable book. Look for insight, foresight, and hindsight. Mentoring is about pointing out what pitfalls to avoid. Instead of a formula, aim for simplicity, commitment, and persistence. Use simplicity in your writings.

How to Motivate People to Interview One Another for Personal History Productions

People are "less camera shy" when two from the same peer group or class pair up and interview each other on video camcorder or on audio tape from a list of questions rehearsed. People also can write the questions they want to be asked and also write out and familiarize themselves with the answers alone and/or with their interviewers from their own peer group.

Some people have their favorite proverbs, or a logo that represents their outlook on life. Others have their own 'crusade' or mission. And some have a slogan that says what they are about in a few words…example, "seeking the joy of life," or "service with a smile."

A play can come from someone's slogan, for example. A slogan, logo, proverb, or motto can form the foundation for a questionnaire on what they want to say in an oral history or personal history video or audio tape on in a multimedia presentation of their life story highlights.

How to Gather Personal Histories

Use the following sequence when gathering oral/aural histories:

1. Develop one central issue and divide that issue into a few important questions that highlight or focus on that one central issue.

2. Write out a plan just like a business plan for your oral history project. You may have to use that plan later to ask for a grant for funding, if required. Make a list of all your products that will result from the oral history when it's done.

3. Write out a plan for publicity or public relations and media relations. How are you going to get the message to the public or special audiences?

4. Develop a budget. This is important if you want a grant or to see how much you'll have to spend on creating an oral history project.

5. List the cost of video taping and editing, packaging, publicity, and help with audio or special effects and stock shot photos of required.

6. What kind of equipment will you need? List that and the time slots you give to each part of the project. How much time is available? What are your deadlines?

7. What's your plan for a research? How are you going to approach the people to get the interviews? What questions will you ask?

8. Do the interviews. Arrive prepared with a list of questions. It's okay to ask the people the kind of questions they would like to be asked. Know what dates the interviews will cover in terms of time. Are you covering the economic depression of the thirties? World Wars? Fifties? Sixties? Pick the time parameters.

9. Edit the interviews so you get the highlights of experiences and events, the important parts. Make sure what's important to you also is important to the person you interviewed.

Document Recovery for Personal History Time Capsules & Memorabilia

How to Open a DNA-Driven Genealogy Reporting and Production Service

How do you rescue and recover memories from mold using conservation techniques? You transport horizontally and store vertically. Store documents and photos in plastic holders, between sheets of waxed paper, or interleave with acid-free paper.

Books are stored spine down. Archive DVDs and CDs in plastic holders and store in plastic crates. To conserve time capsules, according to the American Institute for Conservation of Historic and Artistic Works (AIC), in Washington, DC, neutralize that acid-wracked paper.

Personalize Oral Histories also in Text as Points of View within Social Histories with Corel WordPerfect Office Suite 12 (and beyond).

Preparing Personal History Time Capsules for a Journey

Craft Personal History Time Capsules With DNA Reports Using Corel Graphics Suite and WordPerfect Suite 12 or Beyond.

How to Open Your Own DNA Test Results or Molecular Genealogy Reporting Company—Add DNA-Driven Genealogy Reports to Your Time Capsules.

Use Corel's WordPerfect Office Suite 12 or Beyond to Launch Or Pre-Sell Your Book to the Media Before You Find A Publisher or Agent.

When Your Best Writing Still Isn't Selling, Here Are The Steps To Take: Use your WordPerfect Office Suite for Cover and Follow-Up Letters. The write a fast-selling 98-page pop-culture booklet for store impulse counters.

Writing, Publishing, and Selling Your Own Small Booklets or Pamphlets

Where to Start Your Story

How to Format Your Book Manuscript with Corel WordPerfect Office Suite 12 (and beyond)

How to Write about Your Most Powerful Source

What Do Media Professionals Expect To See?

## Scrap Booking with Poser 5, CorelDRAW! Graphics Suite 12, Word Perfect Office Suite 12, and Beyond.

How to Open Creative Home-Based Businesses Using Poser 5, Corel Graphics, Office Suite 12, and Beyond For Personal Historians, Scrap Bookers and Keepsake Album Crafters: Design your life story in visuals, video, text, and sound with visuals with CorelDRAW Graphics Suite 12, desktop publish with WordPerfect Office 12, and create avatars (or your real photo on an animated figure) with Poser 5.

Use Poser 5 to create avatars or robot characters that move in virtual reality or real time on your DVD, CD, or Web page that can bring to life the photo of your loved one made three dimensional. This 3-D animation and design modeling software creates realistic figures that move, bringing to life for generations into the future your loved on as an avatar or moving animated figure with the real face drawn from an old photo of your loved one as you want to remember him or her. Poser 5 is made by Curious Labs. Check out their software at their Web site at: http://www.curiouslabs.com/

Long after your loved one is gone, you can create new worlds and put the real photo face of your loved on a figure you create or use and change from the software in Poser 5 and beyond. Put the avatar or animated figure in exotic settings or familiar surroundings and centuries. Make a time capsule or a virtual environment as if your own great grandparent or ancestor/ancestral photo or painting was young again and back in the years of his or her youth. That's what a scrap book-keepsake album-time capsule looks like.

You can create an animation video or a still photo in the environment of your creation with Poser 5. Then send your video to the Web or save on a DVD or CD. Use Corel add text, perhaps an Adobe product for DVD editing and desktop publishing, and you have your own animated movie with the real photo face of your loved one or ancestor in a time capsule.

That's what you can do with software and genealogy when you're being a personal historian videographer-desktop publisher multimedia biographer. Let's just call it a time-capsuler or simpler yet, an archivist of personal history.

### How to Make Time Capsules with Corel Graphics Suite 12 and Corel WordPerfect Office Suite 12, and beyond:

**Now you can email your entire scrap book to relatives and friends around the world as time capsules.** Making Time Capsules of family history using graphic design and desktop publishing software? Here's how to create keepsake albums with the same tools graphic designers and desktop publishers use everyday.

Scrap booking newsletters and journals with photos and illustrations online or emailed are becoming popular to send around the world because they weigh nothing. Do your newsletters feature more graphics or text?

If you want to design newsletters, how do you choose between CorelDRAW12 and WordPerfect Office 12? What does CorelDraw Graphics Suite 12 offer the family history newsletter designer, scrap booker, keepsake album crafter, personal historian, and quilter who designs geometric or other art shapes for quilting? How do apply graphics suite software and desktop publishing software programs to home craft projects such as scrap-booking, quilting, personal history documentaries, and time capsules?

How do you compare the two software applications to see which one to buy or both if you want to create newsletters, whether for business or your annual family history time capsules?

"I complete design tasks twice as fast because the tools reduce the number of steps required to finish jobs," says Jim Kendall, of Memory Way Time Capsules, [1] <memoryway@hotmail.com>, a Northern California freelance newsletter designer who specializes in genealogy. "I can create graphics in CorelDRAW12 and quickly pop them into all my text-based WordPerfect 12 office documents because switching between files is very easy.

"The tools reduce the number of times you have to click on your mouse to finish jobs. The reduction in the number of steps is due to the three integrated graphics applications and other tools in one package."

What's the result? Bottom line, it's time saved as well as finger movements on the mouse reduced.

"I like the one-step control of the Smart Drawing tool," says Kendall. "The intelligence recognizes shapes and interprets freehand. My forms are balanced. All I do is put the object where I want it, turn on the Dynamic Guides, and watch the guides change so I can position objects with fewer steps, and snap to different points."

"WordPerfect 12 is for my text material, and CorelDRAW 12 is for my visual work," says Kendall. "Options are important. So that's why I chose WordPerfect Office 12. I generate PDF documents from WordPerfect 12 and Presentations 12 without Adobe Acrobat or other PDF-generating tools. My whole collection of newsletters can be saved as a PDF document or book," says Kendall. "It's important to be able to optimize the size or resolution of PDF files, and WordPerfect Office 12 has a powerful PDF publishing engine."

When you compare CorelDRAW Graphics Suite 12 to WordPerfect Office Suite12, which are best for promoting your writing through newsletters? Both applications are used for creating newsletters. Which one will you use? That depends upon whether you are creating a graphically-rich family history newsletter or time capsule and want to use visual. If your newsletter or time capsule is graphically-rich, CorelDRAW Graphics Suite 12 is the ideal software because it is the easiest graphics suite to use for newsletters or time capsules.

To make a time capsule family history newsletter, layout your page using CorelDRAW. You can layout one page at a time. Then use Corel PHOTO-PAINT for digital imaging, that is working with photos or other digital (electronic, computerized images) art work, illustrations, or photos. What you get in CorelDRAW are hundreds of clip art photos and images. You can overlay your own family photos on top of the clip art textures and images as a second layer to form a background of various places or clouds, for example.

These applications, combined with the suite's vast collection of photos, clipart, and fonts let you design either a professional-looking newsletter or a family history time capsule, a memorable album or container of the highlights of your life or any one else's.

If you don't want to design a lot of visuals into your family history chronicle, use Corel's WordPerfect Office 12 to create a text-based newsletter. Use the software package's newsletter template. It's the best alternative to Microsoft Office. You can use WordPerfect 12 to create that annual family history newsletter that you send out to all your relatives or advertise your genealogy business.

What do you do with all those annual family newsletters you send out to relatives each year at holiday time? Gather them all together from each relative. Newsletters have gone out each year for many years for some families. Put them into a book. One of the best newsletters you can create from family highlights is a book.

Here are several ways of turning family history newsletters into a publication worthy of binding as a book or putting on the Web or in a time capsule as an heirloom:

Take a number of family history newsletters and use Corel's WordPerfect to publish as a PDF file format. In that way, your newsletters are optimized for document distribution, editing, or the Web. You can access family history contact information from your address book directly within WordPerfect 12. Then you can use Perfect-Expert to detail your projects. Create versatile spreadsheets of genealogy time tables or do 3D charting of your family trees.

Convert your family history into meaningful 3D-rendered charts. Use the graphics tools to manipulate photos and drawings or other visuals. Best of all, a family history time capsule or compilation of yearly family history newsletters deserves to add stunning multimedia. Enhance your family newsletter presentation with movies, animation, and MP3 or WMA sounds. It's all done with Corel WordPerfect12.

You can play the slide shows for family members or genealogists or send them to the Web. Use Show on the Go, which is in WordPerfect12. Then publish the slide shows to HTML documents and send them up to the Web for a time capsule in cyberspace online.

What's CorelDRAW? CorelDRAW Graphics Suite is a vector editing program that includes Corel PHOTO-PAINT for bitmap-editing with photos and images that are saved as bitmap image files. How many times have you found photos saved as bitmap images on the Web? Now you can work with photos and images saved as bitmap files using CorelDRAW Graphics Suite.

CorelDRAW 12 for illustration, page-layout and vector drawing includes Corel PHOTO-PAINT 12 for professional digital imaging; and Corel R.A.V.E. 3 for motion-graphics creation. The whole idea is that the new tools emphasize reducing design time so productivity is increased. Users can snap to any or all of the following: Node, Intersection, Midpoint, Quadrant, Tangent, Perpendicular, Edge of objects and lines, Center, Text Baseline or Printable Area.

[1] Memory Way, c/o Writing Courses Online, PO Box 602314, Sacramento, CA 95860 <memoryway@hotmail.com>.

*       *       *

**Where to Find Corel-Approved Training:**

Available in online, printed and CD-ROM formats, WordPerfect Office Suite 12 training resources are provided by highly qualified Corel training partners, all of whom offer customers easy-to-follow instruction on how to maximize their usage of WordPerfect Office 12 the industry's most value-priced, feature-rich Microsoft(R) Office-compatible office suite.

"Corel-approved training tools are the best way to maximize the value of an office suite that's recognized for its ease of use—whether you buy WordPerfect Office 12 in-store, online or bundled with a new computer," said Richard Carriere, General Manager of Office Productivity for Corel. "With over 20 million existing users as well as thousands of new users choosing WordPerfect every month, WordPerfect Office 12 training resources are designed to suit a user's training needs, regardless of their preferred medium."

According to Corel's press release of Sept 7, 2004, Word Perfect Office Suite 12 is available in online, printed and CD-ROM formats. WordPerfect Office Suite 12 training resources are provided by highly qualified Corel training partners, all of whom offer customers easy-to-follow instruction on how to maximize their usage of WordPerfect Office 12—the industry's most value-priced, feature-rich Microsoft® Office-compatible office suite.

"Corel-approved training tools are the best way to maximize the value of an office suite that's recognized for its ease of use—whether you buy WordPerfect Office 12 in-store, online or bundled with a new computer," said Richard Carriere, General Manager of Office Productivity for Corel. "With over 20 million existing users as well as thousands of new users choosing WordPerfect every month, WordPerfect Office 12 training resources are designed to suit a user's training needs, regardless of their preferred medium."

"As the publisher of some of America's most popular training guides, Que Publishing has seen a great increase in the demand to address the growing popularity of WordPerfect Office 12," said Paul Boger, Vice President and Publisher of Que Publishing. "A product as powerful and intuitive as WordPerfect Office 12 provides users with some outstanding benefits, and we're happy to offer two guides that will provide valuable information and help users maximize WordPerfect's potential."

## New WordPerfect Office 12 Training Resources

WordPerfect Office 12 is available coast-to-coast in leading retailers including Office Depot and CompUSA as well as online at leading web retailers including Amazon.com and PCMall.com. The training resources listed below are now available online from their respective publishers:

WordPerfect Office 12 is available coast-to-coast in leading retailers including Office Depot and CompUSA as well as online at leading web retailers including Amazon.com and PCMall.com. The training resources listed below are now available online from their respective publishers:

### —Special Edition Using WordPerfect 12—

Users looking for a complete and up-to-date reference tool brimming with tips, tricks and practical examples, should consider Special Edition Using WordPerfect

12. Available from Que Publishing, this thorough reference guide is for anyone who wants to take advantage of all that WordPerfect 12 has to offer. The book highlights new features and clearly illustrates how to utilize the software fully and effectively. Authors Laura Acklen, a contributing writer for Corel's newsletter, WordPerfect Expert, and Read Gilgen, Director of Learning Support Services at the University of Wisconsin, have both written extensively on WordPerfect.

For more information, visit www.quepublishing.com

*        *        *

Here's how you can use WordPerfect and Corel Graphics suite software together to create your beyond scrap booking business in text and graphics or total multimedia. Using WordPerfect Office Suite 12 or Beyond, Summarize the Highlights or Turning Points and Significant Events in a 7-minute, 1,500 Word Slice-of-Life Vignette. It's direct experience. Put it in a small package and launch it world wide in the media.

**1. Put Direct Experience In A Small Package And Launch It Worldwide.**

**2. Write, Record, & Publish Purpose-Driven Personal History**
**Dramatize, Package, Promote, Present, & Launch Your Purpose**

**3. Edit, Dramatize, Package, Promote, Present, Publish, Record, Produce, & Launch Time Capsules of Personal Histories, Autobiographies, Biographies, Vignettes, and Eulogies and/or DNA-Driven Genealogy Reports: Launching the Inspiration-Driven or Design-Driven Life Story and Detailing Your Purpose.**

If you choose video, the newer camcorders such as Sony brand and others allow you to record directly onto a disk that can be played on a DVD or CD player or saved in the hard disk of a computer. The older camcorders still using tape allow you to save the video on digital high 8 tape and then save the tape in your computer. From there you can record the tape onto a DVD or CD disk.

Have the recording transcribed as text as a backup of information along with photos and other memorabilia for your time capsule. If you're working with tape, you'll need to attach a cable from your camcorder to your computer, such as a 1394 Firewire cable, or other cable device. The cable allows you to capture video and audio from your camcorder and save it in your computer. At the present I'm using Windows XP with Windows Media Player software to capture and edit video and audio.

What do you charge for video recording of personal history? You'd charge similar rates to wedding videographers. Shop around for the current rate in your area as to what wedding videographers charge per hour. Make an affordable, fair budget and present it to your clients. Video is for those who want to be remembered as they look at whatever stage of life they are being recorded.

Clients may also want to edit in youthful video clips, photos, or other memorabilia. Your goal is to make a time capsule with audio, video, photos, memorabilia, and other items such as diaries or DNA-driven ancestry information.

Some videographers charge $100 per hour, plus charges for transcribing video speech as text and saving the text on a CD along with other photo clips and memorabilia inserted into the video recording, such as photos of various stages of life and relatives' photos, video, images, diary excerpts read, or audio clips.

Some clients like to have music inserted. Be sure to obtain a written release from any musicians or composers for use of music on the videos, especially if copies are going to schools, libraries and museums. Check with the music publishers about music clips if the video is only for personal family use.

Some people like to be remembered as they looked when younger and prefer photos with audio. What do you charge for audio? You can charge anywhere from $10 or more to record a one-hour audio life story or oral history on a tape and 'burn' it to a CD or DVD. You can make time capsules by combining photos with the audio on the CD or DVD and make it a multi-media presentation. Or you can transcribe the audio into text.

It takes about five or six hours to transcribe a one-hour tape. Transcribers of tapes usually charge around $20 per hour. Therefore, a one-hour tape that takes five or six hours to transcribe would cost $100–$120 to transcribe. Before you can release a personal history, you'd need to have anyone on tape sign a release form.

Make sure your release form is signed and allows you to copyright the publishing rights to your production. You may not own the person's life story, but you want to make sure that you own the right to publish or produce the tape or disk for educational purposes.

The release form would specify where and how you would use the tape or disk, such as on Web sites or in library archives. Personal history used for educational purposes would be meant for librarians, teachers, students, public historians, and other educators, scholars and researchers. The idea is to share the personal history and create a time capsule—a container for memorabilia—to hand to future generations.

**Personal History Vignettes:**

Put direct experience in a small package and launch it worldwide. Write your life story in short vignettes of 1,500 to 1,800 words.

Write anecdotes, eulogies, vocational biographies, elegies, and vignettes of life stories and personal histories for mini-biographies and autobiographies. Then condense or contract the life stories or personal histories into PowerPoint presentations and similar slide shows on disks using lots of photos and one-page of life story.

Finally, collect lots of vignettes and flesh-out the vignettes, linking them together into first-person diary-style novels and books, plays, skits, or other larger works. Write memoirs or eulogies for people or ghostwrite biographies and autobiographies for others.

If ghostwriting is too invisible, write biographies and vocational biographies, success stories and case histories, and customize for niche interest groups. Your main goal with personal history and life stories is to take the direct experience itself and package each story as a vignette.

The vignette can be read in ten minutes. So fill magazine space with a direct experience vignette. Magazine space needs only 1,500 words. When you link many vignettes together, each forms a book chapter or can be adapted to a play or script.

By turning vignettes into smaller packages, they are easier to launch to the media. When collected and linked together, they form a chain of vignettes offering nourishment, direction, purpose, and information used by people who need to make choices. Here's how to write those inspiration-driven, persistence-driven life stories and what to do with them. Use universal experience with which we all can identify.

Included are a full-length diary-format first person novel and a three-act play, including a monologue for performances. There's a demand for direct life experiences written or produced as vignettes and presented in small packages.

Save those vignettes electronically. Later, they can be placed together as chapters in a book or adapted as a play or script, turned into magazine feature, specialty, or news columns, or offered separately as easy-to-read packages.

## Put Direct Experience In A Small Package And Launch It Worldwide.

*Here's How to Write, Edit, Dramatize, Package, Promote, Present, Publish & Launch Personal Histories, Autobiographies, Biographies, Vignettes, and Eulogies: Launching the Inspiration-Driven or Design-Driven Life Story and Detailing Your Purpose.*

## How to Write Personal History Essays: Text and Audio/Video

Use personal or biographical experiences as examples when you write your essay. Begin by using specific examples taken from your personal experience, personal history, or biographical resources.

Start with a general statement. Then relate the general to your specific personal experience. You don't have to only write about yourself. You can write about someone else as long as you have accurate historical facts about that person, and you state your credible resources.

Here's an example of two opening sentences that state the general and then give the specific personal experience. "Mom's a space garbage woman. She repairs satellites."

Let's analyze all the different parts of an informed argument essay. By analyzing the result in depth instead of only skimming for breadth, you will be able to write concretely from different points of view.

You'll learn how to construct an essay from bare bones—from its concept. You start with a concept. Then you add at least three specific examples to your concept until it develops into a mold. A mold is a form, skeleton or foundation. Think of concept as conception. Think of mold as form or skeleton. Think of awning as the outer skin that covers the whole essay and animates it into lively writing.

You don't want your essay to be flat writing. You want writing that is animated, alive, and able to move, motivate, or inspire readers. Finally, you cover the mold with an awning.

The mold is your pit, skeleton or foundation. Your mold contains your insight, foresight, and hindsight. It has the pitfalls to avoid and the highlights. You need to put flesh on its bones. Then you need to cover your mold with an awning. You need to include or protect that concept and mold or form by including it under this awning of a larger topic or category. The awning holds everything together. It's your category under which all your related topics fall. That's what the technique of organizing your essay or personal history is all about.

In other words, concept equals form plus details. Story equals form plus details. That's the math formula for writing an essay if you'd like to put it into a logical equation of critical thinking. $C = Fo + De$. That's what you need to remember about writing an essay: your concept is composed of your form (mold, foundation, or skeleton) and details. A concept isn't an idea. It's the application of your idea.

A concept is what your story is about. Your concept is imbedded in your story. A story can mean your personal history or any other story or anecdote in your essay, or any highlight of your life or specific life experience. A concept also can be a turning point such as rites of passage or take place at any stage of life.

When writing the informed argument, you will be able to give examples backed up with resources. That's what makes an essay great—knowing what examples to put into the essay at which specific points in time.

Gone will be general, vague, or sweeping statements. Therefore, I'd like each of you on this learning team to start planning your essay by analyzing and discussing the parts that chronologically go into the essay. That's how you organize essays in a linear fashion.

Take an essay apart just as you would take a clock or computer apart, and put it back together. Now all the parts fit and work. Taking apart an essay helps you understand how to plan and write your own essay-writing assignments or personal history as a time capsule.

Here's how to take an essay apart. To analyze an essay in depth, you break the essay down into its six parts: statement-of-position, description, argumentation, exposition, supplementation and evaluation. These parts of an essay also are explained in the book titled, *The Informed Argument.* (**ISBN:** 0155414593).
For more ideas, you also can look at some action verbs in another book titled, *801 Action Verbs for Communicators. (**ISBN**: 0-595-31911-4).

Before you even get to the expressive part of argumentation, you have to state your position and describe it by using specific examples. Then you get to the informed argument in the middle of your essay.

After you've finished arguing logically using critical thinking and your resources, you use exposition. Then you use supplementation, and finally evaluation.

To practice writing personal history essays in text or on video, define and analyze the words 'exposition' and 'supplementation.' Use exposition and supplementation in at least one sentence each as an example of how you would use it in your essay. Don't stick to only what is familiar.

My dictionary defines 'exposition' as "a careful setting out of the facts or ideas involved in something." The principal themes are presented first in a 'music' exposition. Apply it now to an essay. Present your principal themes first in your personal history. Supplementation means adding to your work to improve or complete it.

The goal of an essay is to analyze your informed argument in depth. That's why there are six parts to an essay. Knowing what those six parts are as well as showing examples gives you the experience you need to plan and organize your essay. The result is that once you have organized your plan in writing, the essay almost writes itself.

I keep an old saying in front of me when I write. It's about wanting you to know that I care. You probably want to know that I care more than you care what I know. It's a great saying to remind me why I'm writing how-to books, personal history, writing strategies, plays, and novels…because I care, and because everyone has a life story of great value.

How do you interpret family history as creative writing, and how do you interpret ancestry-related DNA tests?

*       *       *

**Here Are 50 Strategies On How to Write Your Life Story or Anyone Else's:**

**Start with a Vignette….Link the Vignettes…Dramatize….and Novelize.**

1. Contact anyone's family members to gain permission to write their family member's memorials.
2. Write memoirs of various clerical or other religious or social leaders.
3. Write two to four dozen memorials for houses of worship. Put these memorials in a larger book of memoirs for various organizations, religious groups, houses of worship, or professional associations.

4.  Find a model for your biographies.

5.  These could be based on a book of vocational biographies or centered on any other aspect of life such as religious or community service as well as vocations.

6.  Read the various awards biographies written and presented for well-known people.

7.  Focus on the accomplishments that stand out of these people or of you if you're writing an autobiography.

8.  Use oral eulogies as your foundation. You'll find many oral eulogies that were used in memorial services.

9.  Consult professionals who conduct memorial services to look at their eulogies written for a variety of people and presented at memorial services.

10. Stick to the length of a eulogy. You'll find the average eulogy runs about 1,500 to 1,800 words. That' is what's known as magazine article average length. Most magazines ask for feature articles of about 1,500 words. So your eulogies should run that same length.

11. When read aloud, they make up the eulogy part of a memorial service. At 250 to 300 words double-spaced per page, it comes to about five-to-seven pages and is read aloud in about seven to 10 minutes.

12. Take each 1,500–1,800 word eulogy and focus on the highlights, significant events, and turning points. Cut the eulogy down to one page of printed magazine-style format.

13. Keep the eulogy typeset so that it all fits on one page of printed material in 12 point font.

14. You can package one-page eulogies for memorial services or include a small photo on the page if space permits.

15. Cut the eulogy down to 50–70 words, average 60 words for an oral presentation using PowerPoint software for a computer-based slide show complete with photos.

16. Put the PowerPoint show on a CD or DVD. Use the shorter eulogy focusing on significant points in the person's life. The purpose of a PowerPoint eulogy is to show the person lived a purposeful life—a design-driven, goal-driven life with purpose and concrete meaning in relation to others.

17. Write biographies, memoirs, and autobiographies by focusing on the highlights of someone's life or your own life story. Turn personal histories

into life stories that you can launch in the media. You need to make a life story salable. It is already valuable.

18. Read autobiographies in print. Compare the autobiographies written by ghostwriters to those written by the authors of autobiographies who write about their own experiences.

19. Read biographies and compare them to autobiographies written by ghost writers and those written as diary novels in first person or as genre novels in first person. Biographies are written in third person.

20. If you write a biography in third person keep objective. If you write an autobiography in first person you can be subjective or objective if you bring in other characters and present all sides of the story equally.

21. If you're writing a biography, whose memories are you using? If you write an autobiography, you can rely on your own memory. Writing in the third person means research verifying facts and fact-checking your resources for credibility. How reliable is the information?

22. Use oral history transcriptions, personal history, videos, audio tapes, and interviews for a biography. You can use the same for an autobiography by checking for all sides of the story with people involved in the life story— either biography or autobiography.

23. With personal histories and oral histories, be sure to obtain letters of permission and to note what is authorized. Celebrities in the public eye are written about with unauthorized or authorized biographies. However, people in private life who are not celebrities may not want their name or photo in anyone's book. Make sure everything you have is in writing in regard to permissions and what information is permitted to be put into your book or article, especially working with people who are not celebrities and those who are.

24. When interviewing, get written approval of what was said on tape. Let the person see the questions beforehand to be able to have time to recall an answer with accuracy regarding facts and dates or times of various events. Give peoples' memories a chance to recall memories before the interview.

25. Write autobiographies in the first person in genre or diary format. You can also dramatize the autobiography in a play or skit first and then flesh it out into novel format. Another alternative is to focus only on the highlights, events, and turning points in various stages of life.

26. Ghost-written autobiographies usually are written in the first person. A ghost-writer may have a byline such as "*as told to*" or "*with*____(name of ghostwriter)."

27. Condense experience in small chunks or paragraphs. Use the time-capsule approach. Use vignettes. Focus on how people solved problems or obtained results or reached a goal. Find out whether the person wants you to mention a life purpose. Emphasize how the person overcame challenges or obstacles.

28. In an autobiography, instead of dumping your pain on others because it may be therapeutic for you, try to be objective and focus on what you learned from your choices and decisions and how what you learned transformed your life. Be inspirational and nurturing to the reader. Tell how you learned, what you learned, how you rose above your problems, and how you transcended the trouble. Focus on commitment and your relationship to others and what your purpose is in writing the autobiography.

29. Stay objective. Focus on turning points, highlights, and significant events and their relationship to how you learned from your mistakes or choices and rose above the trouble. Decide what your life purpose is and what points you want to emphasize. If you want to hide facts, decide why and what good it will do the reader. Stay away from angry writing and focus instead on depth and analysis.

30. Don't use humor if it puts someone down, including you. Don't put someone down to pick yourself up.

31. Make sure your writing doesn't sound like self-worship or ego soothing. Don't be modest, but don't shock readers either.

32. Before you write your salable autobiography, find out where the market is and who will buy it. If there is no market, use print-on-demand publishing and select a title most likely to be commercial or help market your book. At least you can give copies to friends and family members. Or self-publish with a printer. Another way to go is to self-publish using print-on-demand software yourself. Then distribute via advertising or the Internet and your Web site.

33. You'd be surprised at how many people would be interested in your life story if it were packaged, designed, and promoted. So launch your life story in the media before you publish. Write your life story as a novel or play or both. Every life story has value. I believe all life stories are salable. The hard part is finding the correct niche market for your experiences. So focus on what you are and what you did so people with similar interests,

hobbies, or occupations may learn from you. Market to people who are in the same situation as you are.

34. Divide your biography into the 12 stages of life. Then pare down those 12 significant events or turning points and rites of passage into four quarters—age birth to 25 (young adult), age 26–50 (mature adult), age 51–75 (creative adult) and age 76–100 (golden years of self fulfillment).

35. Start with a vignette focusing on each of the most important events and turning points of your life. Do the same in a biography, only writing in third person. For your own life story, write in first person.

36. What's important for the reader to know about your life in relation to social history and the dates in time? For example, what did you do during the various wars?

37. Keep a journal or diary, and record events as they happen. Focus on how you relate to social history. Write in your diary each day. Use the Web and create a diary or Web *blog*.

38. If you keep a daily journal, and make sure it is saved on a computer disk or similar electronic diary, you can put the whole journal together and create a book or play online or have a digital recording of your life. It's your time capsule in virtual reality.

39. A daily journal will keep memories fresh in your mind when you cut down to significant events for a book. You want to recall significant events in detail with resources.

40. If you're young, keep a daily journal on a computer disk and keep transferring it from one technology to the next as technology evolves. Keep a spare saved and up on the Web so you can download it anytime. Use some of the free Web site space available to people online.

41. If you write a book when you're older, at least you'll have all the youthful memories in detail where you can transfer the notes from one computer to another or upload from your disk to a browser for publication with a print-on-demand publisher.

42. Keep writing short vignettes. Include all the details as soon as possible after the event occurs. When you are ready to write a book, you'll be able to look back rationally and from a much more objective and mature perspective on the details. Then you can decide what to put into a salable life story that's about to be published.

43. Don't listen to people who tell you that if you are not famous, your life story is only fit for your own family because no one else will buy it. Fiddle-de-sticks!

44. There are events that happened to you or experiences in your line of work, travel, parenting, research, or lifestyle that people want to read because you have experiences to share.

45. Find a niche market of people with similar interests and market your life story to them.

46. Try out the waters first with a short vignette in magazines. If the magazines buy your vignette, your slice of life story, then you can write a book. Can you imagine if all the travelers and archaeologists, parenting experts and teachers didn't value their life story to the point that they thought it was fit only for relatives (who may be the only ones not interested in reading it because they already know your life story). In fact, your relatives may be angry at you for spilling the details to the public.

47. Instead, focus on that part of your life where you made a choice or decision with which everyone can identify. Inspire and motivate readers. If your experience is universal, we can all identify with it. We all go through the same stages of life.

48. So let us know how you overcame your obstacles, solved problems, and rose above the keen competition.

49. Or if you didn't, let us know how you learned to live with and enjoy your life. Readers want nourishment. If your life isn't about making a difference in the world, then write about how you handled what we all go through.

50. We want to read about the joy of life, and your design-driven life full of purpose, meaning, and inspiration. We want to read about the universal in you with which we can identify. Most of all readers want information in a life story or personal history from which we can make our own choices. Keep your life story as a novel to 12 to 24 short chapters. Write in short, readable chunks.

# WEEK TWO

## Use Simplicity and Commitment in Personal History Writing or Time Capsules

Here's useful insight to those who may someday write fiction, or their life stories, true experiences, or other people's life stories as vignettes or books created by linking a dozen or more vignettes together into a publishable book. Look for insight, foresight, and hindsight. Mentoring is about pointing out what pitfalls to avoid. Instead of a formula, aim for simplicity, commitment, and persistence. Use simplicity in your writings.

Simplicity means whatever you write gives you all the answers you were looking for in exotic places, but found it close by. This is the formula for selling anything you write, should you desire to send your writing to publishers. You find simplicity in universal proverbs. Then you expand the proverbs to slice-of-life vignettes. Finally, you link those short vignettes.

Suddenly you have a book-length work of writing that can be divided into short vignettes again to be serialized. With most people's attention span set on seven-minutes per vignette, each vignette can emphasize simplicity, commitment, and universal values. Your conclusion would be to focus on answers that can be found close by.

If you're ever looking for 'formulas' in writing any type of literature, this is it: Simplicity shows how you found the answers you were looking for in exotic places but found close by. In your readings you can see the patterns and universals such as commitment that are valued in the story.

You can choose what the writer emphasizes as important. In your own writing, look around for your favorite proverbs and see how you can expand them in your writing to work with your own stories. Enjoy and find wisdom in creative expression. How do you interpret family history as creative writing, and how to you interpret ancestry-related DNA tests?

## What Makes a Personal History or Life Story Highlight Salable as a Play or Skit?

**Q. What makes a life story saleable?**
A. Buzz appeal. High velocity personal memoir. A life story is salable when it has universal appeal and identity. An example is a single parent making great sacrifices to put bread on the table and raise a decent family in hard times. Many people identify with the universal theme of a life story. Buzz appeal draws in the deep interest of the press to publicize and lend credibility to a life story, to put a spin on it in the media, and to sell it to the public because all readers may be able to see themselves in your life story.

**Q. To whom do you sell your life story to?**
A. You sell your life story to publishers specializing in life stories. If you look under biographies in a book such as Writer's Guide to Book Editors, Publishers, and Literary Agents, 1999–2000, by Jeff Herman, Prima Publishing, you'll see several pages of publishers of life story, biography, and memoirs or autobiography.

A few include The Anonymous Press, Andrews McMeel Publishing, Applause Theatre Book Publishers, Barricade Books, Inc., Baskerville Publishers, and many more listed in that directory. Also take a look at Writers Market, Writers Digest Books, checkout Memoirs in the index. Publishers include Feminist Press, Hachai, Hollis, Narwhal, Northeastern University Press, Puppy House, Westminster, John Knox, and others.

Check categories such as creative nonfiction, biography, ethnic, historical, multicultural and other categories for lists of publishers in your genre. Don't overlook writing your life story as a play, monologue, or script or for the audio book market.

**Q. How do you present your life story in order to turn it into a saleable book, article, play, or other type of literature so that other people will want to read it?**
A. You write a high-velocity powerful personal memoir or autonomedia which emphasizes cultural criticism and theory. Or you write a factual expose, keep a journal on the current cultural pulse, or write a diary about what it feels like to be single and dating in your age group—thirty something, sixty-something, or whatever you choose. You become an investigative biographer. You write a riveting love story. Or how to use love to heal. Or you write about breaking through old barriers to create new publishing frontiers.

**Q. How do you write a commercial biography?**
A. Make sure someone wants to buy it before you write the whole thing. The details will be forthcoming in the course as it begins. Then contact the press, reporters in the media with credibility who write for a national daily newspaper or reputable magazine. Also contact radio and cable TV stations to do interviews on a selected event in your life story or biography. Pick a niche market where the particular audience has a special interest in that experience.

**Q. The difference between authorized and unauthorized.**
A. Authorized means you have permission and approval from the person about whom you're writing.

**Q. Who gets assigned to write biographies of celebrities or other famous people?**
A. Usually newspaper columnists who cover the beat or subject area, or you're a known writer who contacts an agent specializing in writing or ghostwriting celebrity biographies. You can enter this profession from many doors. I'll explain in the course.

## Writing Your Ending First Gives You Closure And Clues How To Solve The Problems In Your Life Story. Teaching Life Story Writing On The Internet

When you write a salable life story, it's easier to write your ending first. Eventually, with experience working with a variety of life stories, you can start quality circles or classes in life story writing (writing your salable memoirs, autobiography, biography, corporate history, family history, your diary as a commercial novel or play or true confession, true story, or true crime book or story or script).

Also, you can teach life story writing, interviewing, or videobiography on the Internet for yourself or for an existing school or program. It's relaxing and comforting to sit at home in perfect quiet and type a lecture into a screen browser such as the courses that can be offered through www.blackboard.com and other programs. Or teach online using a live chat screen. Customize your course to the needs of your students.

You may need certification or a graduate degree to teach for a university online, but there's also adult education classes given in nontraditional settings such as churches, libraries, and museums.

Online, you can offer independent classes and go into business for yourself as a personal historian. Another way is to offer time capsules, keepsake albums, gift baskets, greeting cards, life stories on video, DVD, or transcribed from oral history. Work with libraries, museums, or your own independent classes.

You can work at home or be mobile and travel to other people's homes or senior centers and assisted living recreation rooms, community centers, or schools and theaters to work with life stories. Some companies have put life-story recording kiosks in public places such as train stations or airports.

Check out the StoryCorps Web site at http://www.storycorps.net/. Find your own mission or purpose and create your own business recording the life stories of a variety of people in video, sound, text, or multimedia formats. It's all part of the time-capsule generation that emphasizes your life story has value and needs to be preserved as part of history.

The revelation is that your life story isn't only for your family and friends anymore. As part of history, the world can now experience the one universal that connects us—life, and within a life story—insight, foresight, and hindsight.

Diaries of senior citizens are in demand. To sell them, you need buzz appeal, visibility in the press for writing simple stories of how you struggled to put bread on the table and raised a family alone, or what you've learned from your mistakes or experiences, how you solved problems, gave yourself more choices, grew, and came to understand why you were transformed. People are looking for universal experiences to help them make decisions.

Start by finding a newspaper reporter from a publication that is well-respected by the public, and have that person write about your life story experience or what you do with other peoples' life stories as a personal historian. That's the first step to introducing a 'salable' life story.

The technique differs from writing a life story like a first-person diary novel for only your family and/or friends. With a 'salable' life story, you write about the universal experiences that connect all of us. If readers or viewers can identify with what you have to say, your words open doors for them to make decisions and choices by digesting your information.

## The Proliferation of Playwriting Courses Online Targets Writing Your Life Story

The sheer number of classes on the Internet is like an explosion of education. You can now earn a masters degree in the techniques of teaching online from universities such as the California State University at Hayward in their continuing education department. What I see happening is that according to display ads in a variety of magazines of interest to writers, a proliferation of writing courses online has broken out.

How do you develop buzz appeal, pre-sell your book, create press coverage of their writing, all before you send it to a publisher or agent? A few years ago diaries were "in" just like several years before that the books about angels were "in style." What will be next?

Back in the year 2000, what enthralled readers included simple stories on how single parents put bread on the table, reared a family, and learned from their mistakes. What will be big in the future in publishing will be simple tales of what you learned, how you came to understand, and what you'll share with readers because what you learned from my mistakes helped you to grow and become a better person making the world a gentler place. Those books will be about values, virtues, and ethics in simple stories that help people heal. It will be universal stories with which we all can identify and use to solve problems and make decisions.

By the following year books showed readers how to have more choices and find more alternative solutions, more possibilities, and to find more information with which to solve problems and make decisions. A lot of those books will come from salable diaries and life stories as well as corporate histories and executive histories.

What was hot by 2002 was how people escaped domestic violence and made better choices through education and creativity enhancement. By 2003–2004 books focused on creativity enhancement and self-expression. The year 2003 became a utopia for books on creativity enhancement through personal experience and life story. You only have to look at the book lists in the publisher's magazines to see what the fad is for any one year and interview publishing professionals for the trends and directions for the following year.

Write about the human side of careers worked at for years. What did you retire to? How did you survive historic events, rear your family, or solve problems?

The purpose of personal history writing can be, among other goals, to find closure. Those who can't use a hand-operated mouse and need to use a foot pedal mouse, breath straw, or other devices can still operate computers. Others need assistance software to magnify the screen or audio software such as "Jaws," to hear as they type on keyboards.

The idea is to use personal history and life story writing as a healing instrument to make contact with others, find this closure, relieve stress, to talk to parents long gone, to make decisions on how to grow, find understanding, learn from past mistakes, grow, and become a better person in one's own eyes.

Other students take a personal history, oral history, or life story writing classes to pass on to their grandchildren a script, a novel, a story, or a collage of their life experiences, and still others want corporate histories of how they founded their companies and became role models of success for business students to simulate, how they became successful giants for others to follow and benchmark.

Still other students are visionaries who want their life stories to be used to enhance the creativity of readers. Some of my students want to write their life story as a computer or board game on how they solved their own problems that are universal to all of us. And you have students who want careers as personal historians recording, transcribing, and preserving in a variety of formats the personal histories of individuals, families, corporations, art forms, and institutions.

Some are into conservation of videos, photographs, text material, tape recordings, CDs, DVDs, and other multimedia formats. All are involved in making time capsules for future researchers, historians, scholars, librarians, genealogists, and specialists who research personal and oral history or specialized history, such as music and art or rare books and manuscripts.

Others are collectors. Most want a time capsule of a relative, complete with not only a relative's keepsake albums or video diary, but sometimes even a DNA printout for ancestry.

If you look in many publications of interest to writers, you might see online or correspondence courses offered to writers at American College of Journalism, Burlington College, Columbus University, specialists in distance education, or at Gotham Writers' Workshops at www.WritingClasses.com. There's Writers Digest School, and data bases where you can learn about agents at Agent Research & Evaluation, 334 E. 30, NYC, NY 10016 or on the Web at www.agentresearch.com. These are some of the online classes in writing advertised. You'll also see ads for classes in personal story writing in some of these publications.

You can get paid to teach what you love to do so much—share your writing techniques and write. Some writing schools online may put articles up on their trade journal online. And you can always sell articles to paying markets and use the clips with resumes. Thanks to the Internet—even a disabled teacher who isn't able to speak before a class for health reasons or drive to class, can teach and write online.

Personal history writing courses could also aim to show research on how creative writing can heal or have therapeutic qualities in gentle self-expression and quality circles online, and now I've found students who learn how to write a life story as therapy to heal and to find closure, solve problems, and to explore more choices, alternatives, and growth towards a kinder and gentler world.

You can focus strictly on recording, transcribing, and archiving people's or corporation's personal or oral histories and preserving them in a variety of formats as time capsules or target the more creative end of teaching writing personal histories as books, plays, or skits.

In other words, you can be both a personal historian and a writing coach or focus on either career or business—oral and personal historian, or teacher of courses or "quality circles" in writing autobiographies and biographies for commercial markets.

You can start private classes on a mailing list and chat board. A fair price to charge could be about $80 per student for advanced workshops in writing salable material for 4-week courses with a 10-page critique per student. Your aim would be to be an online job coach in a writing or personal history career. Help students find ways to get into print by referring you them to resources. Show how to make writing more commercial. Reveal the techniques of effective story writing in your true story, biography, memoirs, autobiography, diary, journal, novel, story, play, or article.

A lot of biography writing is focused on interviews, whereas writing a diary or monologue focuses on inner reflections and expressions in explaining how you came to understand, learn from your past mistakes or experiences and good choices, and share how you solved problems, grew, and changed or were transformed.

Personal diaries start out with poetic-like descriptions of the senses, with lines such as "Cat shadow plump I arrive, carrying my Siamese kitten like a rifle through Spokane, while the only sensation I feel is my hair stretched like flaxen wires where my new kitten, Patches, hangs on.

A gentle clock, the red beams of light reflected in his blue eyes remind me that my tattered self also must eat. His claws dig into my purse strap like golden flowers curling in unshaven armpits. I inhale his purrs like garlic, warm as the pap mom cat, Rada-Ring flowed into Patches nine weeks ago."

Have an enriching writing experience. I truly believe writing heals in some ways. It's a transformative experience like meditation or having the comforting feeling of watching a waterfall in natural settings or sitting in a garden of hanging green plants. Writing recharges my energy must like petting my kitten, Kokowellen, a Siamese while sitting my orchid garden listening to soothing melodies.

You might want to critique for pay, the pages of other people's writing of personal histories if they want to write for the commercial markets. In that case, critiquing may be done by email and online.

That way they don't send any hard copy to mail back or get lost. You always keep a copy. However, I recommend teaching online a course with the critique, as you'll get far more for your $80 for each ten pages of critiquing as a fair price, plus the tuition of the course as perhaps another $80.

The course provides resources, techniques, and ways to revise your material that helps you gain visibility. It's important to pre-sell your book and gain publicity for your writing before you send it off to a publisher or agent. You'll want to know how not to give too much away, but how to attract positive attention so people will eagerly look forward to hearing more from you.

Keep a separate mailing list for your online students. Make a mailing list. Plays or monologues written from memoirs and diaries or excerpts and highlights of life stories are in right now in the publishing world. It's not a passed fad, yet, like the angel books were a decade ago. If you're writing a diary, you want to write something in your first or second page after the opening that goes like this to be more commercial:

"Eagerness to learn grows on me. I see it reflected in the interviewers who stare at me, their enthusiasm is an approval of my expansive mind. I read so much now, just to look at the pages is to feel nourished. A kind of poetry turns into children's books on DVDs like a stalk that grows no where else is in season.

Creativity, like color, runs off my keyboard into the cooking water of my screen, drenched in pungent brainstorming. Writing online puts me in every farmer's kitchen. My computer has a good scent, and the stories written on its screen are apples bursting on the trees of my fingers. On my Web site, photos hang like lanterns. Teaching online ripens my stories. I analyze what effective storytelling means. Picture in three dimensions, pagodas of the mind."

If you come across writers block, try writing the lyrics to a song as a way to start writing your life story. You don't need to read notes, just fiddle with the words based upon an experience in time. Start by writing the ending first. Perhaps your title on salable diaries could be, "Pretty Little Secret," or "Ending the Silence," or "Results of Promises," or "Guided by a Child's Silence," or "Unraveling a Tale," or "Bravery and Unspeakable Links," or "Unveiled, Unbridled, Unbound." My title was "Insight, Hindsight, Foresight."

Opening Your Online Personal History Business

"Celebration of Life" Plays and Skits Based on Interviewing and Taping:

## How to Motivate People to Interview One Another for Personal History Productions

People are "less camera shy" when two from the same peer group or class pair up and interview each other on video camcorder or on audio tape from a list of questions rehearsed. People also can write the questions they want to be asked and also write out and familiarize themselves with the answers alone and/or with their interviewers from their own peer group.

Some people have their favorite proverbs, or a logo that represents their out-look on life. Others have their own 'crusade' or mission. And some have a slogan that says what they are about in a few words…example, "seeking the joy of life," or "service with a smile."

A play can come from someone's slogan, for example. A slogan, logo, proverb, or motto can form the foundation for a questionnaire on what they want to say in an oral history or personal history video or audio tape on in a multimedia pres-entation of their life story highlights.

Here are some ways to interview people for personal history time capsules or how to inspire them to interview one another in a group setting or in front of a video camcorder in private with only interviewer and interviewee present.

And then there are those who want to tape themselves alone in their room or office with a camcorder on a tripod and a remote control device or a tape recorder and photographs. When records stop, there are always the DNA-driven geneal-ogy and ancestry printouts.

Some people enjoy writing their life stories more than they like to speak about it. Or they prefer to read from a script as an audio tape. For those whose voices are impaired or for those who prefer to let a synthetic software voice tell their story, I recommend software such as TextAloud.

This software allows anyone to cut and paste their writing from a disk such as a floppy disk, CD, DVD, or hard drive disk to the TextAloud software and select the type of voice to read their writing. With AT&T Natural Voices, you can select a male or female voice.

There are also voices with accents, such as a British accent male voice, and voice software available in a variety of languages to read writing in other languages. TextAloud is made by Nextup.com at the Web site: http://www.nextup.com/. According to their Web site, "TextAloud MP3 is Text-to-Speech software that uses voice synthesis to create spoken audio from text. You can listen on your PC or save text to MP3 or wave files for listening later." I play the MP3 files on my MP3 player.

I save the files to a CD as MP3 files. In this way I can turn my writing into audio books, pamphlets, or articles, poetry, plays, monologues, skits, or any form of writing read aloud by the synthetic software voice software. I save my audio files as MP3 files so I can play my personal history audio in my MP3 player on in my personal computer. MP3 files are condensed and take up a lot less room in your computer or on a Web site or CD and DVD disk than an audio .wav file.

For people who are creating "celebration of life" oral or personal history audio tapes, it works well especially for those who prefer not to read their own writing aloud to a tape recorder. Although most people would like to hear their relatives' voices on tape in audio and video, some people are not able to read their works aloud to a recorder or camcorder.

The synthetic voices will turn any type of writing saved on a disk as a text file into recorded voice—from short poetry to long-length books. The voices are usually recorded with Total Recorder software and saved as an MP3 file so they can be played on MP3 players or on most computers with CD players.

For those taping persons live in video to make time capsules or other keepsake albums in voice and/or video, it's best to let people think what they are going to say by handing them a list of a few questions. If you're working with a group of older adults, let one of the group members interview another group member by asking each question from a list of several questions.

If you give someone a week's notice to come up with an answer to each question from a list of ten questions and give them two minutes to respond to each question by discussing how it relates to events in their lives or their experiences, you have a twenty minute video tape.

If you allow only a minute for each question from a list of thirty questions, you have a thirty-minute tape. Times may not be exact as people tend to elaborate to flesh out a question. Let the interview and interviewee practice before recording. So it's good to pair up two people. One will ask the interview questions, and the other will answer, talking about turning points and significant events in their lives.

They can be asked whether they have a personal proverb or slogan they live by or a motto or personal logo. Tapes can be anywhere from a half hour to an hour for life stories that can be saved as an MP3 file to a CD. Other files such as a Wave file (.wav) take up too much space on a CD. So they could be condensed into an MP3 file and saved that way. TextAloud and Total Recorder are software programs that save audio files. You can also use Music Match to convert .wav files to MP3 files.

I use TextAloud software and Total Recorder. Also I save the files as MP3 files for an audio CD that will also go up on a Web site. I use Windows Media Player to play the video files and save them as a Windows Media file (WMV file) so they can be easily uploaded to a Web site and still play in Windows Media Player that comes with Windows XP software.

When making time capsules in multimedia, I save on a CD and/or a DVD, and upload the file from my hard disk to a Web site. Copies of the CDs can be given to relatives, the interviewee, museums, libraries, and various schools who may be interested in oral history with a theme.

The themes can be celebrations of life, living time capsules, or fit into any group theme under an umbrella title that holds them together. This can be an era, such as living memories of a particular decade, life experiences in oral history of an area in geography, an ethnic group, or any other heading. Or the tapes can be of individuals or family groups.

Not only life stories, but poetry, plays, novels, stories, and any other form of creative nonfiction or fiction writing can be recorded by synthetic voices as audio story or book collections. Some work well as children's stories and other types of writings as life stories or poetry.

Themes can vary from keepsake albums to time capsules to collections of turning points in history from the life stories of individuals. Also, themes can be recorded as "old time radio" programs or as oral military history from the experiences of veterans and notated to the Veterans History Project at the Library of Congress or other groups and museums. Make sure you have signed *release forms* that also release you from liability should any problems arise from putting someone's life story and name on the Web and/or donating it to a library or other public archive.

A good example of a release form is the one posted at the Veteran's History Project Web site where life stories of veterans are donated to the Library of Congress and accessible to the public for educational or scholarly research. Check out the .PDF release forms for both the interviewer and the interviewee at their Web site. The release form for veterans is at: http://www.loc.gov/folklife/vets/vetform-vetrelease.pdf.

\*       \*       \*

## Before Video Taping Life Stories of Older Adults: Questions to Ask

### Interviewing for Writing Plays and Skits from Life Stories for Junior and Senior High-School Students and/or Mature Adults.

STEP 1: Send someone enthusiastic about personal and oral history to senior community centers, lifelong learning programs at universities, nursing homes, or senior apartment complexes activity rooms. You can reach out to a wide variety of older adults in many settings, including at libraries, church groups, hobby and professional or trade associations, unions, retirement resorts, public transportation centers, malls, museums, art galleries, genealogy clubs, and intergenerational social centers.

STEP 2: Have each personal historian or volunteer bring a tape recorder with tape and a note pad. Bring camcorders for recording video to turn into time capsules and CDs or DVDs with life stories, personal history experiences, memoirs, and events highlighting turning points or special times in people's lives.

STEP 3: Assign each personal historian one or two older persons to interview with the following questions.

1. What were the most significant turning points or events in your life?

2. How did you survive the Wars?

3. What were the highlights, turning points, or significant events that you experienced during the economic downturn of 1929–1939? How did you cope or solve your problems?

4. What did you do to solve your problems during the significant stages of your life at age 10, 20, 30, 40, 50, 60 and 70-plus? Or pick a year that you want to talk about.

5. What changes in your life do you want to remember and pass on to future generations?

6. What was the highlight of your life?

7. How is it best to live your life after 70?

8. What years do you remember most?

9. What was your favorite stage of life?

10. What would you like people to remember about you and the times you lived through?

STEP 3:

Have the student record the older person's answers. Select the most significant events, experiences, or turning points the person chooses to emphasize. Then write the story of that significant event in ten pages or less.

STEP 4: Ask the older person to supply the younger student photos, art work, audio tapes, or video clips. Usually photos, pressed flowers, or art work will be supplied. Have the student or teacher scan the photos onto a disk and return the original photos or art work or music to the owner.

STEP 5: The personal historian, volunteer, student and/or teacher scans the photos and puts them onto a Web site on the Internet at one of the free communities that give away Web site to the public at no cost....some include http://www.tripod.com, http://www.fortunecity.com, http://www.angelfire.com, http://www.geocities.com, and others. Most search engines will give a list of communities at offering free Web sites to the public. Microsoft also offers free family Web sites for family photos and newsletters or information. Ask your Internet service provider whether it offers free Web site space to subscribers. The free Web sites are limited in space.

For larger Web site spaces with room for audio and video material and other keepsake memorabilia, purchase a personal Web site from a Web-hosting company. Shop around for affordable Web site space for a multimedia life story time capsule that would include text, video and/or audio clips, music, art, photos, and any other effects.

1. Create a Web site with text from the older person's significant life events

2. Add photos.

3. Add sound or .wav files with the voice of the older person speaking in small clips or sound bites.

4. Intersperse text and photos or art work with sound, if available.

Add video clips, if available and won't take too much bandwidth.

5. Put Web site on line as TIME CAPSULE of (insert name of person) inter-viewed and edited by, insert name of student who interviewed older person.

STEP 6: Label each Web site Time Capsule and collect them in a history archives on the lives of older adults at the turn of the millennium. Make sure the older person and all relatives and friends are emailed the Web site link. You have now created a time capsule for future generations.

This can be used as a classroom exercise in elementary and high schools to teach the following:

1.  Making friends with older adults.
2.  Learning to write on intergenerational topics.
3.  Bringing community together of all generations.
4.  Learning about foster grandparents.
5.  History lessons from those who lived through history.
6.  Learning about diversity and how people of diverse origins lived through the 20th century.
7.  Preserving the significant events in the lives of people as time capsules for future generations to know what it was like to live between 1900 and 2000 at any age.
8.  Learning to write skits and plays from the life stories of older adults taken down by young students.
9.  Teaching older adults skills in creative writing at senior centers.
10. Learning what grandma did during World War 2 or the stock market crash of 1929 followed by the economic downturn of 1930–1938.

**What to Ask People about Their Lives before You Write a Play or Skit**

Step 1

When you interview, ask for facts and concrete details. Look for statistics, and research whether statistics are deceptive in your case.

Step 2

To write a plan, write one sentence for each topic that moves the story or piece forward. Then summarize for each topic in a paragraph. Use dialogue at least in every third paragraph.

Step 3

Look for the following facts or headings to organize your plan for a biography or life story.

1. PROVERB. Ask the people you interview what would be their proverb or slogan if they had to create/invent a slogan that fit themselves or their aspirations: One slogan might be something like the seventies ad for cigarettes, "We've come a long way, baby," to signify ambition. Only look for an original slogan.

2. PURPOSE. Ask the people you interview or a biography, for what purpose is or was their journey? Is or was it equality in the workplace or something personal and different such as dealing with change—downsizing, working after retirement, or anything else?

3. IMPRINT. Ask what makes an imprint or impact on people's lives and what impact the people you're interviewing want to make on others?

4. STATISTICS: How deceptive are they? How can you use them to focus on reality?

5. How have the people that you're interviewing influenced changes in the way people or corporations function?

6. To what is the person aspiring?

7. What kind of communication skills does the person have and how are these skills received? Are the communication skills male or female, thinking or feeling, yin or yang, soft or steeled, and are people around these people negative or positive about those communication skills?

8. What new styles is the person using? What kind of motivational methods, structure, or leadership? Is the person a follower or leader? How does the person match his or her personality to the character of a corporation or interest?

9. How does the person handle change?

10. How is the person reinforced?

Once you have titles and summarized paragraphs for each segment of your story, you can more easily flesh out the story by adding dialogue and description to your factual information. Look for differences in style between the people you interview? How does the person want to be remembered?

Is the person a risk taker or cautious for survival? Does the person identify with her job or the people involved in the process of doing the work most creatively or originally?

Does creative expression take precedence over processes of getting work out to the right place at the right time? Does the person want his ashes to spell the words "re-invent yourself" where the sea meets the shore? This is a popular concept appearing in various media.

## Search the Records in the Family History Library of Salt Lake City, Utah

Make use of the database online at the Family History Library of Salt Lake City, Utah. Or visit the branches in many locations. The Family History Library (FHL) is known worldwide as the focal point of family history records preservation.

The FHL collection contains more than 2.2 million rolls of microfilmed genealogical records, 742,000 microfiche, 300,000 books, and 4,500 periodicals that represent data collected from over 105 countries. You don't have to be a member of any particular church or faith to use the library or to go online and search the records.

Family history records owe a lot to the invention of writing. And then there is oral history, but someone needs to transcribe oral history to record and archive them for the future.

Interestingly, isn't it a coincidence that writing is 6,000 years old and DNA that existed 6,000 years ago first reached such crowded conditions in the very cities that had first used writing extensively to measure accounting and trade had very little recourse but to move on to new areas where there were far less people and less use of writing?

A lot of major turning points occurred 6,000 years ago—the switch to a grain-based diet from a meat and root diet, the use of bread and fermented grain beverages, making of oil from plants, and the rise of religions based on building "god houses" in the centers of town in areas known as the "cereal belt" around the world.

Six thousand years ago in India we have the start of the Sanskrit writings, the cultivation of grain. In China, we have the recording of acupuncture points for medicine built on energy meridians that also show up in the blue tattoos of the Ice Man fossil "Otsi" in the Alps—along the same meridians as the Chinese acupuncture points.

At 6,000 years ago the Indo European languages spread out across Europe. Mass migrations expanded by the Danube leaving pottery along the trade routes that correspond to the clines and gradients of gene frequency coming out of the cereal belts.

Then something happened. There was an agricultural frontier cutting off the agriculturists from the hunters. Isn't it a coincidence that the agricultural frontiers or barriers also are genetic barriers at least to some degree?

## Oral History

Here's how to systematically collect, record, and preserve living peoples' testimonies about their own experiences. After you record in audio and/or video the highlights of anyone's experiences, try to verify your findings. See whether you can check any facts in order to find out whether the person being recorded is making up the story or whether it really did happen.

This is going to be difficult unless you have witnesses or other historical records. Once you have verified your findings to the best of your ability, note whether the findings have been verified. Then analyze what you found. Put the oral history recordings in an accurate historical context.

Mark the recordings with the dates and places. Watch where you store your findings so scholars in the future will be able to access the transcript or recording and convert the recording to another, newer technology. For instance, if you have a transcript on paper, have it saved digitally on a disk and somewhere else on tape and perhaps a written transcript on acid-free good paper in case technology moves ahead before the transcript or recording is converted to the new technology.

For example, if you only put your recording on a phonograph record, within a generation or two, there may not be any phonographs around to play the record. The same goes for CDs, DVDs and audio or video tapes.

So make sure you have a readable paper copy to be transcribed or scanned into the new technology as well as the recordings on disk and tape. For example, if you record someone's experiences in a live interview with your video camera, use a cable to save the video in the hard disk of a computer and then burn the file to a CD or DVD.

Keep a copy of audio tape and a copy of regular video tape—all in a safe place such as a time capsule, and make a copy for various archives in libraries and university oral history preservation centers. Be sure scholars in the future can find a way to enjoy the experiences in your time capsule, scrapbook, or other storage device for oral histories.

Use your DNA testing results to add more information to a historical record. As an interviewer with a video camera and/or audio tape recorder, your task is to record as a historical record what the person who you are interviewing recollects.

The events move from the person being interviewed to you, the interviewer, and then into various historical records. In this way you can combine results of DNA testing with actual memories of events. If it's possible, also take notes or have someone take notes in case the tape doesn't pick up sounds clearly.

I had the experience of having a video camera battery go out in spite of all precautions when I was interviewing someone, and only the audio worked. So keep a backup battery on hand whether you use a tape recorder or a video camera. If at all possible, have a partner bring a spare camera and newly recharged battery. A fully charged battery left overnight has a good chance of going out when you need it.

## Writing Skits from Oral and Personal History Transcripts

Emphasize the commitment to family and faith. To create readers' and media attention to an oral history, it should have some redemptive value to a universal audience. That's the most important point. Make your oral history simple and earthy. Write about real people who have values, morals, and a faith in something greater than themselves that is equally valuable to readers or viewers.

Publishers who buy an oral history written as a book on its buzz value are buying simplicity. It is simplicity that sells and nothing else but simplicity. This is true for oral histories, instructional materials, and fiction. It's good storytelling to say it simply.

Simplicity means the oral history or memoirs book or story gives you all the answers you were looking for in your life in exotic places, but found it close by. What's the great proverb that your oral history is telling the world?

Is it to stand on your own two feet and put bread on your own table for your family? That's the moral point, to pull your own weight, and pulling your own weight is a buzz word that sells oral histories and fiction that won't preach, but instead teach and reach through simplicity.

That's the backbone of the oral historian's new media. Buzz means the story is simple to understand. You make the complex easier to grasp. And buzz means you can sell your story or book, script or narrative by focusing on the values of simplicity, morals, faith, and universal values that hold true for everyone.

Doing the best to take care of your family sells and is buzz appeal, hot stuff in the publishing market of today and in the oral history archives. This is true, regardless of genre. Publishers go through fads every two years—angel books, managing techniques books, computer home-based business books, novels about ancient historical characters or tribes, science fiction, children's programming, biography, and oral history transcribed into a book or play.

The genres shift emphasis, but values are consistent in the bestselling books. Perhaps your oral history will be simple enough to become a bestselling book or script. In the new media, simplicity is buzz along with values.

Oral history, like best-selling novels and true stories is built on simplicity, values, morals, and commitment. Include how one person dealt with about trends. Focus your own oral history about life in the lane of your choice. Develop one central issue and divide that issue into a few important questions that highlight or focus on that one central issue.

When you write or speak a personal history either alone or in an interview, you focus on determining the order of your life story. Don't use flashbacks. Focus on the highlights and turning points. Organize what you'll say or write. An autobiography deals in people's relationships. Your autobiography deals as much with what doesn't change—the essentials—as what life changes you and those around you go through.

Your personal history should be more concrete than abstract. You want the majority of people to understand what you mean. Say what you mean, and mean what you say. More people understand concrete details than understand abstract ideas.

## How to Gather Personal Histories

**Use the following sequence when gathering oral/aural histories:**

10. Develop one central issue and divide that issue into a few important questions that highlight or focus on that one central issue.

11. Write out a plan just like a business plan for your oral history project. You may have to use that plan later to ask for a grant for funding, if required. Make a list of all your products that will result from the oral history when it's done.

12. Write out a plan for publicity or public relations and media relations. How are you going to get the message to the public or special audiences?

13. Develop a budget. This is important if you want a grant or to see how much you'll have to spend on creating an oral history project.

14. List the cost of video taping and editing, packaging, publicity, and help with audio or special effects and stock shot photos of required.

15. What kind of equipment will you need? List that and the time slots you give to each part of the project. How much time is available? What are your deadlines?

16. What's your plan for a research? How are you going to approach the people to get the interviews? What questions will you ask?

17. Do the interviews. Arrive prepared with a list of questions. It's okay to ask the people the kind of questions they would like to be asked. Know what dates the interviews will cover in terms of time. Are you covering the economic depression of the thirties? World Wars? Fifties? Sixties? Pick the time parameters.

18. Edit the interviews so you get the highlights of experiences and events, the important parts. Make sure what's important to you also is important to the person you interviewed.

19. Find out what the interviewee wants to emphasize perhaps to highlight events in a life story. Create a video-biography of the highlights of one person's life or an oral history of an event or series of events.

20. Process audio as well as video, and make sure you have written transcripts of anything on audio and/or video in case the technology changes or the tapes go bad.

21. Save the tapes to compact disks, DVDs, a computer hard disk and several other ways to preserve your oral history time capsule. Donate any tapes or CDs to appropriate archives, museums, relatives of the interviewee, and one or more oral history libraries. They are usually found at universities that have an oral history department and library such as UC Berkeley and others.

22. Check the Web for oral history libraries at universities in various states and abroad.

23. Evaluate what you have edited. Make sure the central issue and central questions have been covered in the interview. Find out whether newspapers or magazines want summarized transcripts of the audio and/or video with photos.

24. Contact libraries, archives, university oral history departments and relevant associations and various ethnic genealogy societies that focus on the subject matter of your central topic.

25. Keep organizing what you have until you have long and short versions of your oral history for various archives and publications. Contact magazines and newspapers to see whether editors would assign reporters to do a story on the oral history project.

26. Create a scrapbook with photos and summarized oral histories. Write a synopsis of each oral history on a central topic or issue. Have speakers give public presentations of what you have for each person interviewed and/or for the entire project using highlights of several interviews with the media for publicity. Be sure your project is archived properly and stored in a place devoted to oral history archives and available to researchers and authors.

## Aural/Oral History Techniques

1. Begin with easy to answer questions that don't require you explore and probe deeply in your first question. Focus on one central issue when asking questions. Don't use abstract questions. A plain question would be

"What's your purpose?" An abstract question with connotations would be "What's your crusade?" Use questions with denotations instead of connotations. Keep questions short and plain—easy to understand. Examples would be, "What did you want to accomplish? How did you solve those problems? How did you find closure?" Ask the familiar "what, when, who, where, how, and why."

2. First research written or visual resources before you begin to seek an oral history of a central issue, experience, or event.

3. Who is your intended audience?

4. What kind of population niche or sample will you target?

5. What means will you select to choose who you will interview? What group of people will be central to your interview?

6. Write down how you'll explain your project. Have a script ready so you don't digress or forget what to say on your feet.

7. Consult oral history professionals if you need more information. Make sure what you write in your script will be clear to understand by your intended audience.

8. Have all the equipment you need ready and keep a list of what you'll use and the cost. Work up your budget.

9. Choose what kind of recording device is best—video, audio, multimedia, photos, and text transcript. Make sure your video is broadcast quality. I use a Sony Digital eight (high eight) camera.

10. Make sure from cable TV stations or news stations that what type of video and audio you choose ahead of time is broadcast quality.

11. Make sure you have an external microphone and also a second microphone as a second person also tapes the interview in case the quality of your camera breaks down. You can also keep a tape recorder going to capture the audio in case your battery dies.

12. Make sure your battery is fully charged right before the interview. Many batteries die down after a day or two of nonuse.

13. Test all equipment before the interview and before you leave your office or home. I've had batteries go down unexpectedly and happy there was another person ready with another video camera waiting and also an audio tape version going.

14. Make sure the equipment works if it's raining, hot, cold, or other weather variations. Test it before the interview. Practice interviewing someone on

your equipment several times to get the hang of it before you show up at the interview.

15. Make up your mind how long the interview will go before a break and use tape of that length, so you have one tape for each segment of the interview. Make several copies of your interview questions.

16. Be sure the interviewee has a copy of the questions long before the interview so the person can practice answering the questions and think of what to say or even take notes. Keep checking your list of what you need to do.

17. Let the interviewee make up his own questions if he wants. Perhaps your questions miss the point. Present your questions first. Then let him embellish the questions or change them as he wants to fit the central issue with his own experiences.

18. Call the person two days and then one day before the interview to make sure the individual will be there on time and understands how to travel to the location. Or if you are going to the person's home, make sure you understand how to get there.

19. Allow yourself one extra hour in case of traffic jams.

20. Choose a quiet place. Turn off cell phones and any ringing noises. Make sure you are away from barking dogs, street noise, and other distractions.

21. Before you interview make sure the person knows he or she is going to be video and audio-taped.

22. If you don't want anyone swearing, make that clear it's for public archives and perhaps broadcast to families.

23. Your interview questions should follow the journalist's information-seeking format of asking, who, what, where, where, how, and why. Oral history is a branch of journalistic research.

24. Let the person talk and don't interrupt. You be the listener and think of oral history as aural history from your perspective.

25. Make sure only one person speaks without being interrupted before someone else takes his turn to speak.

26. Understand silent pauses are for thinking of what to say.

27. Ask one question and let the person gather his thoughts.

28. Finish all your research on one question before jumping to the next question. Keep it organized by not jumping back to the first question after the second is done. Stay in a linear format.

29. Follow up what you can about any one question, finish with it, and move on to the next question without circling back. Focus on listening instead of asking rapid fire questions as they would confuse the speaker.

30. Ask questions that allow the speaker to begin to give a story, anecdote, life experience, or opinion along with facts. Don't ask questions that can be answered only be yes or no. This is not a courtroom. Let the speaker elaborate with facts and feelings or thoughts.

31. Late in the interview, start to ask questions that explore and probe for deeper answers.

32. Wrap up with how the person solved the problem, achieved results, reached a conclusion, or developed an attitude, or found the answer. Keep the wrap-up on a light, uplifting note.

33. Don't leave the individual hanging in emotion after any intensity of. Respect the feelings and opinions of the person. He or she may see the situation from a different point of view than someone else. So respect the person's right to feel as he does. Respect his need to recollect his own experiences.

34. Interview for only one hour at a time. If you have only one chance, interview for an hour. Take a few minutes break. Then interview for the second hour. Don't interview more than two hours at any one meeting.

35. Use prompts such as paintings, photos, music, video, diaries, vintage clothing, crafts, antiques, or memorabilia when appropriate. Carry the photos in labeled files or envelopes to show at appropriate times in order to prime the memory of the interviewee. For example, you may show a childhood photo and ask "What was it like in that orphanage where these pictures were taken?" Or travel photos might suggest a trip to America as a child, or whatever the photo suggests. For example, "Do you remember when this ice cream parlor inside the ABC movie house stood at the corner of X and Y Street? Did you go there as a teenager? What was your funniest memory of this movie theater or the ice cream store inside back in the fifties?"

36. As soon as the interview is over, label all the tapes and put the numbers in order.

37. A signed release form is required before you can broadcast anything. So have the interviewee sign a release form before the interview.

38. Make sure the interviewee gets a copy of the tape and a transcript of what he or she said on tape. If the person insists on making corrections, send

the paper transcript of the tape for correction to the interviewee. Edit the tape as best you can or have it edited professionally.

39. Make sure you comply with all the corrections the interviewee wants changed. He or she may have given inaccurate facts that need to be corrected on the paper transcript.

40. Have the tape edited with the corrections, even if you have to make a tape at the end of the interviewee putting in the corrections that couldn't be edited out or changed.

41. As a last resort, have the interviewee redo the part of the tape that needs correction and have it edited in the tape at the correct place marked on the tape. Keep the paper transcript accurate and up to date, signed with a release form by the interviewee.

42. Oral historians write a journal of field notes about each interview. Make sure these get saved and archived so they can be read with the transcript.

43. Have the field notes go into a computer where someone can read them along with the transcript of the oral history tape or CD.

44. Thank the interviewee in writing for taking the time to do an interview for broadcast and transcript.

45. Put a label on everything you do from the interview to the field notes. Make a file and sub file folders and have everything stored in a computer, in archived storage, and in paper transcript.

46. Make copies and digital copies of all photos and put into the records in a computer. Return originals to owners.

47. Make sure you keep your fingerprints off the photos by wearing white cotton gloves. Use cardboard when sending the photos back and pack securely. Also photocopy the photos and scan the photos into your computer. Treat photos as antique art history in preservation.

48. Make copies for yourself of all photos, tapes, and transcripts. Use your duplicates, and store the original as the master tape in a place that won't be used often, such as a time capsule or safe, or return to a library or museum where the original belongs.

49. Return all original photos to the owners. An oral history archive library or museum also is suitable for original tapes. Use copies only to work from, copy, or distribute.

50. Index your tapes and transcripts. To use oral history library and museum terminology, recordings and transcripts are given "accession numbers."

51. Phone a librarian in an oral history library of a university for directions on how to assign accession numbers to your tapes and transcripts if the materials are going to be stored at that particular library. Store copies in separate places in case of loss or damage.

52. If you don't know where the materials will be stored, use generic accession numbers to label your tapes and transcripts. Always keep copies available for yourself in case you have to duplicate the tapes to send to an institution, museum, or library, or to a broadcast company.

53. Make synopses available to public broadcasting radio and TV stations.

54. Check your facts.

55. Are you missing anything you want to include?

56. Is there some place you want to send these tapes and transcripts such as an ethnic museum, radio show, or TV satellite station specializing in the topics on the tapes, such as public TV stations? Would it be suitable for a world music station? A documentary station?

57. If you need more interviews, arrange them if possible.

58. Give the interviewee a copy of the finished product with the corrections. Make sure the interviewee signs a release form that he or she is satisfied with the corrections and is releasing the tape to you and your project.

59. Store the tapes and transcripts in a library or museum or at a university or other public place where it will be maintained and preserved for many generations and restored when necessary.

60. You can also send copies to a film repository or film library that takes video tapes, an archive for radio or audio tapes for radio broadcast or cable TV.

61. Copies may be sent to various archives for storage that lasts for many generations. Always ask whether there are facilities for restoring the tape. A museum would most likely have these provisions as would a large library that has an oral history library project or section.

62. Make sure the master copy is well protected and set up for long-term storage in a place where it will be protected and preserved.

63. If the oral history is about events in history, various network news TV stations might be interested. Film stock companies may be interested in copies of old photos.

64. Find out from the subject matter what type of archives, repository, or storage museums and libraries would be interested in receiving copies of the oral history tapes and transcripts.

65. Print media libraries would be interested in the hard paper copy transcripts and photos as would various ethnic associations and historical preservation societies. Find out whether the materials will go to microfiche, film, or be digitized and put on CDs and DVDs, or on the World Wide Web. If you want to create a time capsule for the Web, you can ask the interviewee whether he or she wants the materials or selected materials to be put online or on CD as multimedia or other. Then you would get a signed release from the interviewee authorizing you to put the materials or excerpts online. Also find out in whose name the materials are copyrighted and whether you have print and electronic rights to the material or do the owners-authors-interviewees—or you, the videographer-producer? Get it all in writing, signed by those who have given you any interviews, even if you have to call your local intellectual property rights attorney.

## Document Recovery for Personal History Time Capsules & Memorabilia

How do you rescue and recover memories from mold using conservation techniques? You transport horizontally and store vertically. Store documents and photos in plastic holders, between sheets of waxed paper, or interleave with acid-free paper. Books are stored spine down. Archive DVDs and CDs in plastic holders and store in plastic crates. To conserve time capsules, according to the American Institute for Conservation of Historic and Artistic Works (AIC), in Washington, DC, neutralize that acid-wracked paper.

### Diaries, Bibles, and Old Family Cookbooks

Here's how to "mend conditions" and restore diaries. First make a book jacket for a diary. Put a title and label on the dust jacket with the name of the diary's author and any dates, city, state, or country.

Use acid-free paper for the jacket. Diaries and book jackets are works of art. If torn, mend the diary. Apply a protective plastic wrapper to your valuable dust jacket or give diaries dust jackets in good condition.

Be cautious using bleach, because chlorine fumes will fade the ink and soak through the opposite page to fade that writing. After testing the bleach, if the diary is dingy and dirty, bleach it white on the edges only using diluted bleach that won't fade old ink. Test the bleach first on similar surfaces, such as a blank page in the book.

Repair old diaries, and turn them into heirlooms for families and valuable collectibles. The current price for repairing handwritten diaries and books is about $50 and up per book or bound diary. Better yet, publish diaries as print-on-demand PDF files and print them out as paperback books with covers for families.

Some diaries served as handwritten cookbooks containing recipes created by a particular family cook. For more repair tips on bound diaries-as-cook-books, I recommend the book titled, *How to Wrap a Book*, Fannie Merit Farmer, Boston Cooking School.

How do you repair an old diary or family recipe book to make it more valuable to heirs? You'll often find a bound diary that's torn in the seams. According to Barbara Gelink, of the 1990s Collector's Old Cookbooks Club, San Diego, to repair a book, you take a bottle of Book Saver Glue (or any other book-repairing or wood glue), and spread the glue along the binder.

Run the glue along the seam and edges. Use wax paper to keep the glue from getting where it shouldn't. Put a heavy glass bottle on the inside page to hold it down while the glue dries.

Use either the *finest* grade sand paper or nail polish remover to unglue tape, tags, or stains from a *glossy* cover. Sit away from heat, light, and sparks. Carefully dampen a terry cloth with nail polish remover, lighter, or cleaning fluid and circle gently until the tag and stain are gone. On a *plastic* book cover, use the finest grade of sandpaper.

Memorabilia such as diaries, genealogy materials, books, photos, ivory, sports trophies, cards, discarded library and school books, or fabrics that end up at estate sales or thrift shops may have adhesive price tags.

To bleach the "discarded book stamp" that libraries and schools often use, or any other rubber stamp mark, price, date, or seals on the pages or edges, use regular bleach, like Clorox. It turns the rubber stamp mark white. The household bleach also turns the edges and pages of the book white as new.

To preserve a valuable, tattered dust jacket with tears along the edges, provide extra firmness. Put a protective plastic wrapper on top of the book jacket cover of a diary, especially if it's handwritten.

To collect diaries or family photos, look in garage sales, flea markets, and antique shops. Attend auctions and book fairs. Two recommended auction houses for rare cookbooks include Pacific Book Auction Galleries, 139 Townsend, #305, San Francisco, CA 94107, or Sotheby's, New York, 1334 York Ave., New York, NY 10021. Pacific Book Auction Galleries sometimes puts cookbook collections up for an auction.

Look for old high-school graduation class year books to collect from various high schools or middle schools found in garage and estate sales. Restore them and find out whether there's an alumni association whose members want that book stored where all can access it, such as in a public or school library offering interstate library loans.

Can the diary, recipe book, or school yearbook be restored and digitized on DVDs with permission from those who copyrighted it? If you're into keepsake album making with family history photos, diaries, or recipes, look for cookbooks printed by high school parent-teacher associations. Some old ones may be valuable, but even the one put out by the depression era San Diego High School Parent Teacher Association for the class of 1933–34 is only worth $10.

You can start a family history business specializing in restoring diaries, domestic history journals, school yearbooks, and certain types of personal, rare, or cook books. For example, *Cornucopia*, run by Carol A. Greenberg, has old and rare books emphasizing cooking, food literature, domestic history, household management, herbs, kitchen gardens, hotels, restaurants, etiquette, manners, pastimes, amusements, and needlework.

They search for out-of-print books, and are interested in material from the 19th century through 1940. Write to: Little Treasures at PO Box 742, Woodbury, NY 11797. Greenberg is always grateful for quotations on old, rare, and unusual materials in fine condition.

You could start a collector's old diaries and photos club. Marge Rice is a pioneer genealogist who created a hobby of returning heirloom photos to their families of origin. See the related article at: http://www.ancestry.com/library/view/ancmag/7643.asp. Or digitize photos for the Web. See the instructional site on digitizing photos for the Web at: http://www.firstmonday.dk/issues/issue8_1/garner/.

Some bound, handwritten diaries were purchased as blank or lined notebooks. People who collect autographs may also be interested in diaries of authors. For example, the published diary novel titled *One Day Some Schlemiel Will Marry Me* is a diary that ended up as a published first person life story novel. Other diaries end up as cookbooks.

Are diaries worth as much as rare cookbooks? How much are the thousands of rare cookbooks worth today? A helpful guide is the Price Guide to Cookbooks & Recipe Leaflets, 1990, by Linda J. Dickinson, published by Collector Books, at PO Box 3009, Paducah, KY 42002-3009.

See Bibliography of American Cookery Books, 1742–1860. It's based on Waldo Lincoln's American Cookery Books 1742–1860, by Eleanor Lowenstein. Over 800 books and pamphlets are listed. Order from Oak Knoll Books & Press, 414 Delaware St., Newcastle, Delaware 19720.

Louis & Clark Booksellers specialize in rare and out-of-print cookery, gastronomy, wine and beverages, baking, restaurants, domestic history, etiquette, and travel books. They're at 2402 Van Hise Avenue, Madison, WI 53705. Cook books are much more in demand than diaries, unless the author has celebrity status.

Make copies of diaries. Work with the photocopies when you decipher the writing. Store your old diaries in a dry, cool place. Lining the storage place with plastic that's sealed will keep out vermin, moisture, and bugs. Without moisture, you can keep out the mildew and mold. Store duplicates away from originals.

Was something placed in a diary on a certain page, such as a dried rose, letter, farmer's wheat stain, or a special book mark? What meaning did it have? Look for clues for a time frame. Date the diary. List the date it was begun and when it was ended if you can. List the geographic location of the events in the diary and the writer's travels.

Of what kind of materials is the diary made? Is it improvised, created at low cost by the author? Or is it fancy and belonging to someone of wealth? What is the layout like? Does it show the education of the writer or anything personal? Was it a farmer's almanac, captain's log or sailor's calendar, personal journal or if recent, a Web log (blog)?

What was the writing tool, a quill or a pencil? What's the handwriting like? What century or years? Is it full of details, maps, corsages, and pictures? What is its central message? Do you see patterns or mainly listed facts?

Transcribe the diary with your computer. Read it into a camcorder or on audio tape. It's now oral history. What historical events influenced the writing of the diary? What's the social history? What language is it in or dialect? Are there vital records such as wills or deeds to real estate mentioned in the diary? You've now mended, restored, and conserved a life story and a pattern on the quilt of humanity.

## Acid Paper:

Here's how to prevent acidic paper damage in your paper memorabilia or on your items stored against paper. According to author, Betty Walsh, Conservator, BC Archives, Canada and the Walsh's information at: http://palimpsest.stanford.edu/waac/wn/wn10/wn10-2/wn10-202.html, use acid-free paper around photos. To store paper that has a high acid content, put the papers in folders and storage boxes with an alkaline reserve to prevent acid migration. Interleave your papers with sheets of alkaline-buffered paper.

The buffered paper protects your item from acids that move from areas of high to areas of low concentration. Buffers neutralize acids in paper. A buffer is an alkaline chemical such as calcium carbonate. So you have the choice to use the buffered or non-buffered paper depending on whether your photos are stored against other acid-free materials or printed on acid-free paper.

## Photos:

Interweave photos with waxed paper or polyester web covered blotters. Store photos away from overhead water pipes in a cool, dry area with stable humidity and temperatures, not in attics or basements. Keep photos out of direct sunlight and fluorescent lights when on display. Color slides have their own storage requirements.

Keep photos from touching rubber bands, cellophane tape, rubber cement, or paper clips. Poor quality photo paper and paper used in most envelopes and album sleeves also cause photos to deteriorate. Instead, store photos in chemically stable plastic made of polyester, polypropylene, triacetate, or polyethylene. Don't use PCV or vinyl sleeves. Plastic enclosures preserve photos best and keep out the fingerprints and scratches.

Albumen prints are interleaved between groups of photographs. Matte and glossy collodion prints should not be touched by bare hands. Store the same as albumen prints—interleaved between groups of photos. Silver gelatin printing and developing photo papers are packed in plastic bags inside plastic boxes. Carbon prints and Woodbury prints are packed horizontally. Photomechanical prints are interleaved every two inches and packed in boxes. Transport color photos horizontally—face up.

Chromogenic prints and negatives are packed in plastic bags inside boxes. If you're dealing with cased photos, pack the ambrotypes and pannotypes horizontally in padded containers. Cover the glass of Daguerreotype photos and pack horizontally in padded containers.

Pollutants from the air trapped inside holders and folders destroy photos and paper. Use buffered enclosures for black and white prints and negatives. Use non-buffered paper enclosures to store color prints and color print negatives or cyanotypes and albumen prints.

Store your tintypes horizontally. If you have collodion glass plate negatives, use supports for the glass and binders, and pack horizontally in padded containers. The surface texture of photos stored in plastic can deteriorate. It's called ferrotyping. So don't store negatives in plastic. If you store your photos in paper enclosures, be aware that paper is porous. Instead of plastic or paper storage, put photos in *glass plate negative sleeves in acid-free non-buffered enclosures.*

Then store vertically between pieces of foam board. Where do you find glass plate negative sleeves that can be stored in acid-free non-buffered enclosures? Buy storage materials from companies catering to conservationists, such as *Light Impressions* ®. They're the leading resource for archival supplies. Also look in local craft stores.

Talk to your state archives conservation specialist. Some documents require the work of a trained conservationist. Before you sterilize mold away with bleach, ask your state archives conservationist whether the bleach will ruin your diary or heirloom.

**Photo Albums:**

Don't make or buy photo albums with "peel-back" plastic over sticky cardboard pieces because they are chemically unstable and could damage anything stored there. Instead, use photo-packet pages made from chemically stable plastic made of polyester, polypropylene, triacetate, or polyethylene. An excellent album would contain archival-quality pages using polyester mounting corners. Acid-free paper mounting corners are next best.

## Vellum or Parchment Documents:

Interleave between folders, and pack oversize materials flat. If you have prints and drawings made from chemically stable media, then interleave between folders and pack in cartons. Oversize prints and drawings should be packed in bread trays, or map drawers, placed on poly-covered plywood. Be careful the mildew from plywood doesn't paste onto the back of your print. Look at the poly-covering on the wood.

Take off the frames of your drawings or prints if you can. Books with leather and vellum bindings need to be packed spine down in crates one layer deep. Books and pamphlets should be separated with freezer paper and always packed spine down in crates one layer deep.

Bread trays work well to store parchment and vellum manuscripts that are interleaved between folders. Anything oversize gets packed flat. Posters need to be packed in containers lined with garbage bags because they are *coated* papers. Watercolors and hand-colored prints or inks should be interleaved between folders and packed in crates. Paintings need to be stored *face up* without touching the paint layer. Carry them horizontally.

## Computer Tapes and Disks, Audio and Video Tapes:

Store those 'dinosaur' computer tapes in plastic bags packed vertically with plenty of room. Store in plastic crates away from light, heat, or cold. Never touch the magnetic media. If you have an open reel tape, pick up by the hub or reel. Floppy disks should be packed vertically in plastic bags and stored in plastic crates.

With DVDs and CDs, pack vertically in plastic crates and store in plastic drawers or cardboard cartons. Careful—don't touch or scratch the recordable surface. Handle the CD or DVD by the edge. Place audio and video tapes vertically in plastic holders and store them in plastic crates.

Disks made of shellac or acetate and vinyl disks are held by their edges and packed vertically in ethafoam-padded crates. Make sure nothing heavy is placed on CDs, DVDs, tapes, or other disks. You can find ethafoam in most craft stores, or order from a company specializing in storage and presentation tools such as Light Impressions. ®

\*          \*          \*

## Resources:

American Institute for Conservation
1717 K Street, NW, Suite 200
Washington, DC 20006
tel: 202-452-9545
fax: 202-452-9328
email: info@aic-faic.org
website: http://aic.stanford.edu

Light Impressions (Archival Supplies)
PO Box 22708
Rochester, NY 14692-2708
1-800-828-6216
http://www.lightimpressionsdirect.com

## Bibliography:

**WAAC Newsletter**
http://palimpsest.stanford.edu/aic'disaster
WAAC Newsletter, Vol. 19, No 2 (May, 1997) articles and charts online by Betty
Walsh, Conservator, BC Archives, Canada and the Walsh's information at:
http://palimpsest.stanford.edu/waac/wn/wn10/wn10-2/wn10-202.html. The site
contains material from the WAAC Newsletter, Volume 10, Number 2, May
1988, pp.2–5.

Curatorial Care of Works of Art on Paper, New York: Intermuseum Conservation
Association, 1987.

Library Materials Preservation Manual: Practical Methods for Preserving Books,
Pamphlets, and Other Printed Materials, Heidi Kyle. 1984

Archives & Manuscripts: Conservation—A Manual on Physical Care and
Management, Mary Lynn Ritzenthaler, Society of American Archivists: Chicago,
1993.

## Personalize Oral Histories also in Text as Points of View within Social Histories with Corel WordPerfect Office Suite 12 (and beyond).

Autobiographies, biographies, personal histories, plays, and monologues present a point of view. Are all sides given equal emphasis? Will the audience choose favorite characters? Cameras give fragments, points of view, and bits and pieces. Viewers will see what the videographer or photographer intends to be seen. The interviewee will also be trying to put his point of view across and tell the story from his perspective.

Will the photographer or videographer be in agreement with the interviewee? Or if you are recording for print transcript, will your point of view agree with the interviewee's perspective and experience if your basic 'premise,' where you two are coming from, are not in agreement? Think this over as you write your list of questions. Do both of you agree on your central issue on which you'll focus for the interview?

How are you going to turn spoken words into text for your paper hard copy transcript? Will you transcribe verbatim, correct the grammar, or quote as you hear the spoken words? Oral historians really need to transcribe the exact spoken word. You can leave out the 'ahs' and 'oms' or loud pauses, as the interviewee thinks what to say next. You don't want to sound like a court reporter, but you do want to have an accurate record transcribed of what was spoken.

You're also not editing for a movie, unless you have permission to turn the oral history into a TV broadcast, where a lot gets cut out of the interview for time constraints. For that, you'd need written permission so words won't be taken out of context and strung together in the editing room to say something different from what the interviewee intended to say.

Someone talking could put in wrong names, forget what they wanted to say, or repeat themselves. They could mumble, ramble, or do almost anything. So you would have to sit down and weed out redundancy when you can or decide on presenting exactly what you've heard as transcript.

When someone reads the transcript in text, they won't have what you had in front of you, and they didn't see and hear the live presentation or the videotape.

It's possible to misinterpret gestures or how something is spoken, the mood or tone, when reading a text transcript. Examine all your sources. Use an ice-breaker to get someone talking.

If a woman is talking about female-interest issues, she may feel more comfortable talking to another woman. Find out whether the interviewee is more comfortable speaking to someone of his or her own age. Some older persons feel they can relate better to someone close to their own age than someone in high school, but it varies. Sometimes older people can speak more freely to a teenager.

The interviewee must be able to feel comfortable with the interviewer and know he or she will not be judged. Sometimes it helps if the interviewer is the same ethnic group or there is someone present of the same group or if new to the language, a translator is present.

Read some books on oral history field techniques. Read the National Genealogical Society Quarterly (NGSQ). Also look at The American Genealogist (TAG), The Genealogist, and The New England Historical and Genealogical Register (The Register). If you don't know the maiden name of say, your grandmother's mother, and no relative knows either because it wasn't on her death certificate, try to reconstruct the lives of the males who had ever met the woman whose maiden name is unknown.

Maybe she did business with someone before marriage or went to school or court. Someone may have recorded the person's maiden name before her marriage. Try medical records if any were kept. There was no way to find my mother's grandmother's maiden name until I started searching to see whether she had any brothers in this country. She had to have come as a passenger on a ship around 1880 as she bought a farm. Did her husband come with her?

Was the farm in his name? How many brothers did she have in this country with her maiden surname? If the brothers were not in this country, what countries did they come from and what cities did they live in before they bought the farm in Albany? If I could find out what my great grandmother's maiden name was through any brothers living at the time, I could contact their descendants perhaps and see whether any male or female lines are still in this country or where else on the globe.

Perhaps a list of midwives in the village at the time is recorded in a church or training school for midwives. Fix the person in time and place. Find out whom she might have done business with and whether any records of that business exist. What businesses did she patronize? Look for divorce or court records, change of name records, and other legal documents.

Look at local sources. Did anyone save records from bills of sale for weddings, purchases of homes, furniture, debutante parties, infant supplies, or even medical records? Look at nurses' licenses, midwives' registers, employment contracts, and teachers' contracts, alumni associations for various schools, passports, passenger lists, alien registration cards, naturalization records, immigrant aid societies, city directories, and cross-references.

Try religious and women's clubs, lineage and village societies, girl scouts and similar groups, orphanages, sanatoriums, hospitals, police records. Years ago there was even a Eugenics Record Office. What about the women's prisons? The first one opened in 1839—Mount Pleasant Female Prison, NY.

Try voters' lists. If your relative is from another country, try records in those villages or cities abroad. Who kept the person's diaries? Have you checked the Orphan Train records? Try ethnic and religious societies and genealogy associations for that country. Most ethnic genealogy societies have a special interest group for even the smallest villages in various countries.

You can start one and put up a Web site for people who also come from there in past centuries. Check alimony, divorce, and court records, widow's pensions of veterans, adoptions, orphanages, foster homes, medical records, birth, marriage, and death certificates, social security, immigration, pet license owners' files, prisons, alumni groups from schools, passenger lists, military, and other legal records.

When all historical records are being tied together, you can add the DNA testing to link all those cousins. Check military pensions on microfilms in the National Archives. See the bibliography section of this book for further resources on highly recommended books and articles on oral history field techniques and similar historical subjects.

# WEEK SEVEN

## Preparing Personal History Time Capsules for a Journey

Use Corel Graphics Suite 12 and beyond to create images so you can become more visual as well as more personal in a personal history life story. Use the text and oral form of a personal history. Then insert visual images and video clips among the highlights of the text.

The more personal you are, the more eternal is your life story. More people will view or read it again and again far into the future. You can emphasize your life's journey and look at the world through your own eyes. To make the structure salable, 'meander' your life as you would travel on a journey. Perhaps you're a winding river meandering around obstacles and competitors. At each stop, you learn your own capabilities and your own place in the world.

The more you meander, the more you take away the urgency from your story that sets up tension in the audience and keeps them on the edge of their seat. Don't let the meandering overpower your sense of urgency. Don't dwell on your reaction. Focus on your action to people and situations. Stay active in your own personal history. In other words, don't repeat how you reacted, but show how you acted.

Before you sit down to write your autobiography, think of yourself in terms of going on a journey inside the privacy of your purse or wallet. May your purse is the only place where you really do have any privacy. Come up for air when you have hit bottom. Bob up to the sunshine, completely changed or at least matured.

If you have really grown, you will not be blinded by the light, in the figurative sense, as the song goes. Instead, the light gives you insight. So now you have vision along with some hindsight. The next step is learning how to promote and market your salable personal history or life story.

A biography reports the selected events of another person's life—usually 12 major events in the six various significant events also known as "turning points" and also known as "transition points" of life that would include the highlights of significant events for each of the six stages of growth: 1) infanthood, 2) childhood, 3) teen years 4) young adulthood 5) middle life 6) maturity.

## Selling Life Stories

Launch your salable life story in the major national press and in various newspapers and magazines of niche markets related to the events in your life, such as weekly newspapers catering to a group: senior citizens, your ethnic group, your local area, or your occupation or area of interest. Your personal history time capsule may be saved to disk and also uploaded to the Web. What about looking for movie deals and book publishers?

If you don't have the money to produce your autobiography as a video biography, or even a film or commercial movie, or publish it for far less cost as a print-on-demand published book, you may wish to find a co-production partner to finance the production of your life story as a cinematic film or made-for-TV video.

At the same time you could contact literary agents and publishers, but one front-page article in a national newspaper or daily newspaper can do wonders to move your life story in front of the gaze of publishers and producers. While you're waiting for a reporter to pay attention to the news angle you have selected for your life story, I highly recommend Michael Wiese's book <u>Film and Video Marketing</u> because it lists some co-production partners as the following:

Private Investors/Consortiums
Foreign Governments (blocked funds)
Financiers
Corporations
Theatrical Distributors
International Theatrical Distributors
International Sales Agents
Home Video
International Home Video
Pay TV
Syndicators
Record Companies
Music Publishers
Book Publishers
Toy Companies
Licensing and Merchandising Firms
Sponsors (products, services)
Public Relations Firms

Marketing Companies/Consultants
Film Bookers

You can also contact actors, directors, producers, feature distributors, home video distributors, entertainment lawyers, brokers, accountants, animation houses, production houses, video post production houses, labs, film facilities, and agents with your script and ask the owners whether they'd be interested in bartering budget items, deferring, or investing in your script.

Private investors could also be professional investors, venture capitalists, and even doctors and dentists who may wish to finance a movie if the potential interests them. You can sell points in your film to investors who finance it as a group of investors, each buying a small percentage of the film for an investment fee.

Or you can approach film investment corporations that specialize in investing in and producing films as partners. They are publicized or listed in the entertainment trade magazines going to producers and workers in the entertainment and film or video industry.

You market your script not only to agents and producers, but to feature distributors, film financiers and co-production partners. This is the first step in finding a way to take your autobiography from script to screen. Learn who distributes what before you approach anyone.

If you want to approach video instead of film, you might wish to know that children's video programming is the fastest-growing genre in original programming. Children's titles account for 10%-15% of the overall home video revenues. According to one of Michael Wiese's books written in the nineties, *Home Video: Producing For The Home Market*, "With retail prices falling and alternative retail outlets expanding, children's programming will soon become one of the most profitable segments of the video market." He was right.

What has happened in the new millennium is that children's program is doing wonderfully. Why? Children's video is repeatable. Children watch the same tape 30 to 50 times. Children's video sells for comparatively lower prices than feature films.

Children's video also rents well. Children's tapes sell it toy stores, book stores, children's stores, and in stores like Woolworth's and Child World. Manufacturers sell tapes at Toy Fair and the American Booksellers Association conventions.

For these reasons, you may wish to write your autobiography as a script for children's video or as a children's book. Video is a burgeoning industry.

According to the market research firm, Fairfield Group, in 1985, the prerecorded video business earned $ 3.3 billion in sales and rentals. This nearly equaled the record and theatrical box office revenues for the same year. The world

VCR population is about 100 million. Today we have the DVD and the Internet streaming video.

Back in 1985, the U.S. and Japan accounted for half of the VCRs, followed by the United Kingdom, (9 million) West Germany (nearly 7 million), and Canada, Australia, Turkey, and France (about 3 million each). Spain reported 2 million VCRs. By 1991, the number of VCR ownership increased as prices slowly came down.

Today, in the 21st century, the prerecorded video business has quickly moved to DVD disks, downloadable at a price Internet-based movies, and video tapes are on the way to being a memory of the eighties and early nineties. In the next decade, another media format will be in fashion to replace videos on DVDs and streaming Internet video. The idea is to keep transferring the story from one form of technology to another so that videos made today will be able to be viewed by people in the next century.

The European VCR markets grew faster than in the U.S. during the eighties and nineties just as the DVD markets grew in the early 21st century because there were fewer entertainment alternatives—fewer TV stations, restricted viewing hours, fewer pay TV services, and fewer movie theatres.

You should not overlook the foreign producers for your script. Include Canadian cable TV, foreign agents, and foreign feature film and video producers among your contacts. Most university libraries open to the public for research include directories listing foreign producers. Photocopy their addresses and send them a query letter and one-page synopsis of your script. Don't overlook the producers from non-English speaking countries. Your script can be translated or dubbed.

You might attend film market type conventions and conferences. They draw producers from a variety of countries. In 1989 at the former Cinetex Film Market in Las Vegas, producers from Canada, Italy, Israel, Spain, and other foreign countries sat next to script writers. All of them were receptive to receiving scripts. They handed one another their business cards. You can learn a lot at summer film markets and film festivals about what kind of scripts are in demand.

Keep a list of which film markets will meet. In the U.S. there are 3 to 5 film markets a year and many more film festivals. Seek out the foreign and local producers with track records and see whether they'd be interested in your script if you have a life story in the form of a script, treatment, or story. Perhaps your theme has some relation to a producer's country or ethnic group. Lots of films are made in Asia, in the Middle East (Israel, Egypt and Tunisia), in Latin America, and Europe or Canada.

Seek out the Australian producers also and New Zealand or India. If you have a low-budget film or home video script set in Korea, Philippines, Japan, or

Taiwan, or a specialty film such as Karate or something that appeals to the Indian film market, contact those producers and script agents in those countries. Find out the budget limitations that producers have in the different countries.

Social issues documentaries based on your autobiography are another market for home video. Vestron and other home video distributors use hard-hitting documentaries. Collecting documentary video tapes is like collecting copies of <u>National Geographic</u> magzine. You never throw them out. Tapes are also sold by direct mail. Companies producing and distributing documentaries include MCA, MGM/UA, Vestron, Victory, CBS/Fox, Warner, Media, Karl, Monterey, Thorn/EMI, Embassy, and USA, to name a few.

If you write your autobiography or another's biography as a romance, you might wish to write a script for the video romance series market. Romance video has its roots in the paperback novel. However, the biggest publishers of romance novels have little recognition in retail video stores.

Among consumers, yes; wholesalers and retailers, no. Bookstores, yes. The problem is with pricing. To sell romance videos in bookstores, the tapes would have to be sold at less than $29. In video stores, they can be positioned the same as $59 feature films on video.

Production costs to make high quality romance videos are high. Top stars, top writers, hit book titles, exotic locations, music and special effects are required. Huge volumes of tapes must be sold to break even. Then producers have to search for pay TV, broadcast, or foreign partners. The budget for a one-hour video tape of a thin romance story comes to $500,000.

It's far better to make a low-budget feature film. Romance as a genre has never previously appealed to the video retail buyer. In contrast, a romance paperback sells for a few dollars. Now the question remains: Would women buy a romance-genre video DVD priced at $9.95?

Romance novels successfully have been adapted to audio tape for listening at far less than the cost of video. There is a market for audio scripts of short romance novels and novellas. What is becoming popular today are videos and 'movies' downloadable from the Internet that you can watch on your computer screen or save to a DVD since DVD burners became affordable and popular. Try adapting highlights of your romance or life story novel to a play, skit, or monologue.

The only way romance videos would work is by putting together a multi-partnered structure that combines pay TV, home video, book publishing, and domestic and foreign TV. In the eighties, was anyone doing romance video tapes? Yes. Prism Video produced six feature-length romance films, acquired from Comworld. In 1985 the tapes sold for $11.95.

Comworld had limited TV syndication exposure and was one of the first to come out with romance videos. Karl/Lorimar came out with eight romance films from L/A House Productions on a budget of $400,000 each. They were also priced at $11.95 in 1985. To break even, a company has to sell about 60,000 units per title.

Twenty years later, think about adapting to a play the romance DVD video and the downloadable Internet video. What's available to adapt as educational material? Write for various age groups on niche subjects that would appeal to teachers. Follow their rules on what is appropriate for their classrooms. The market also is open for stage and radio/Internet broadcast skits and plays geared to older adults as performers and audiences.

Other media are like open doors to finding a way to put your life story on a disk. Any interview, script, or story can go from print-on-demand published novel or true story book to radio script or stage play. A video can move from a digital high 8 camcorder with a Firewire 1394 cable attached to a personal computer rapidly into the hard disk drive via Windows XP Movie Maker software. Or you can purchase the latest camcorders that record directly onto a mini-disk that looks similar to a small CD or DVD and which can be played directly on your CD or DVD player or saved and played in your computer.

From there it can be saved as a WMV file (a Windows Media file). Then the file can be recorded on a DVD, if long, or a CD if under one hour. Poems can be written, read, and 'burned' to a compact disk (CD) and then mailed out as greeting cards, love letters, or personal histories. Short videos can be emailed.

Romance or life story highlights novels and scripts on audio tape cost less to produce. This market occasionally advertises for romantic novel manuscripts, scripts, and stories in a variety of writer's magazines.

Check out the needs of various magazines for journalists and writers online. If you read a lot of romance genre novels or write in this style, you may want to write your autobiography in this genre, but you'd have to market to publishers who use this genre or biographies in other genres such as factual biography.

If your autobiography is set on events which occurred in your childhood, you might prefer to concentrate on writing appropriate for children's video programming. It's a lot easier to sell to the producers who are basking in the current explosion of children's video programming. Perhaps it's your mission to use the video format to teach children.

### Will the script of your life story do the following?

teach,

mentor,

motivate,

inspire,

or inform viewers who can be:

children,

teenagers,

parents

or midlifers on their quests for self-identify:

or in their search for facts:

to use as guidelines in making their own decisions:

about life's journeys and writing an introspective journal?

Can your diary be dynamic, dramatic, and empowering to others who may be going through similar stages of life? Are your characters charismatic and memorable, likable and strong?

A life story or autobiography when videotaped or filed as a feature-length movie can spring out of a diary or an inner personal journal (which dialogues with the people who impact your life and observes selected, important events).

Craft Personal History Time Capsules With DNA Reports Using Corel Graphics Suite and WordPerfect Suite 12 or Beyond.

How to Open Your Own DNA Test Results or Molecular Genealogy Reporting Company—Add DNA-Driven Genealogy Reports to Your Time Capsules.

Did you ever wonder what you can do with Corel Graphics Suite and WordPerfect 12 other than compare them? You can use them to illustrate and express yourself in images, photos, and words as the next money-making step as a scrap booker and personal historian. Become an entrepreneur for genealogists. Genealogy is about searching records for family history and ancestry.

So you be the crafter and wholesale supplier of images and text to genealogists and DNA-driven genealogy companies. It's about opening a genealogy-driven DNA testing service. Take your pick: tracking ancestry by DNA for pets or people. You don't need any science courses or degrees to start or operate this small business. It can be done online, at home, or in an office. What should you charge per test? About $200 is affordable. You'll have to pay a laboratory to do the testing. Work out your budget with the laboratory.

Laboratories that do the testing can take up to fifty percent of what you make on each test unless they have research grants to test a particular ethnic group and need donors to give DNA for testing. Each lab is different. Shop around for an affordable, reputable laboratory. Your first step would be to ask the genetics and/or molecular anthropology departments of universities who's applying for a grant to do DNA testing. Also check out the oral history libraries which usually are based at universities and ethnic museums. You're bringing together two different groups—genealogists and geneticists.

You'd work with the laboratories that do the testing. Customers want to see online message boards to discuss their DNA test results and find people whose DNA sequences match their own.

So you'd need a Web site with databases of the customers, message boards, and any type of interactive communication system that allows privacy and communication. DNA database material would not show real names or identify the people. So you'd use numbers. Those who want to contact others could use regular email addresses. People want ethnic privacy, but at the same time love to find DNA matches. At this point you might want to work only with dogs, horses, or other pets or farm animals providing a DNA testing service for ancestry or nutrition.

Take your choice as an entrepreneur: sending the DNA of people to laboratories to be tested for ancestry or having the DNA of dogs, horses or other pets and animals sent out to be tested for ancestry and supplying reports to owners regarding ancestry or for information on how to tailor food to the genetic signatures of people or animals. For animals, you'd contact breeders.

For people, your next step is to contact genealogists and genealogy online and print publications. You'd focus on specific ethnic groups as a niche market. The major groups interested in ancestry using DNA testing include Northern European, Ashkenazi, Italian, Greek, Armenian, Eastern European, African, Asian, Latin American, and Middle Eastern.

Many successful entrepreneurs in the DNA testing for ancestry businesses started with a hobby of looking up family history records—genealogy. So if you're a history buff, or if your hobby is family history research, oral history, archaeology, or genealogy, you now can turn to DNA testing.

What you actually sell to customers are DNA test kits and DNA test reports. To promote your business, offer free access to your Web site database with all your clients listed by important DNA sequences.

Keep names private and use only assigned numbers or letters to protect the privacy of your clients. Never give private and confidential genetic test information to insurance companies or employers. Clients who want to have their DNA tested for ancestry do not want their names and DNA stored to fall into the "wrong hands." So honor privacy requests. Some people will actually ask you to store DNA for future generations.

If you want to include this service, offer a time capsule. For your clients, you would create a time capsule, which is like a secure scrap book on acid-free paper and on technology that can be transferred in the future when technology changes. Don't store anything on materials that can't be transferred from one technology to another. For example, have reports on acid-free paper.

You can include a CD or DVD also, but make sure that in the future when the CD players aren't around any longer, the well-preserved report, perhaps laminated or on vellum or other acid-free materials that don't crumble with age can be put into the time capsule. You can include a scrap book with family photos and video on a CD if you wish, or simply offer the DNA test report and comments explaining to the customer what the DNA shows.

Use plain language and no technical terms unless you define them on the same page. Your goal is to help people find other people who match DNA sequences and to use this knowledge to send your customers reports. If no matches can be found, then supply your clients with a thorough report. Keep out any confusing jargon. Show with illustrations how your customer's DNA was tested. In plain language tell them what was done.

Your report will show the results, and tell simply what the results mean. You can offer clients a list of how many people in what countries have their same DNA sequences. Include the present day city or town and the geographic location using longitude and latitude. For example, when I had my mtDNA (maternal lineages) tested, the report included my DNA matches by geographic coordinates. The geographic center is 48.30N 4.65E, Bar sur Aube, France with a deviation of 669.62 miles as done by "Roots for Real," a London company that tests DNA for ancestry. The exact sequences are in the Roots for Real Database (and other mtDNA databases) for my markers.

You're going to ask, with no science background yourself, how will you know what to put in the report? That's the second step. You contact a university laboratory that does DNA testing for outside companies. They will generate all the reports for you. What you do with the report is to promote it by making it look visually appealing. Define any words you think the customer won't understand with simpler words that fully explain what the DNA sequences mean and what the various letters and numbers mean. Any dictionary of genetic terms will give you the meaning in one sentence using plain language. Use short sentences in your reports and plain language.

Your new service targets genealogists who help their own customers find lost relatives. Your secondary market is the general public. Most people taking a DNA test for ancestry want information on where their DNA roamed 20,000 years ago and in the last 10,000 years. DNA testing shows people only where their ancient ancestors camped. However, when sequences with other people match exactly, it could point the way to an ancient common ancestor whose descendants went in a straight line from someone with those sequences who lived 10,000 years ago to a common ancestor who lived only a few generations ago.

Those people may or may not actually be related, but they share the same sequences. The relationship could be back in a straight line 20,000 years or more or only a few centuries. Ancient DNA sequences are spread over a huge area, like mine—from Iceland to Bashkortostan in the Urals. DNA sequences that sprung up only a few generations ago generally are limited to a more narrow geographic area, except for those who lived in isolation in one area for thousands of years, such as the Basques.

You would purchase wholesale DNA kits from laboratory suppliers and send the kits to your customer. The customer takes a painless cheek scraping with a felt or cotton type swab or uses mouthwash put into a small container to obtain DNA that can help accurately determine a relationship with either a 99.9% probability of YES or a 100% certainly that no near term relationship existed.

The DNA sample is sealed and mailed to a laboratory address where it is tested. The laboratory then disposes of the DNA after a report is generated. Then you package the report like a gift card portfolio, a time capsule, or other fancy packaging to look like a gift. You add your promotional material and a thorough explanation of what to expect from the DNA test—the results.

The best way to learn this business is to check out on the Web all the businesses that are doing this successfully. Have your own DNA tested and look at the printout or report of the results. Is it thorough? Does it eliminate jargon? Include in the report materials the client would like to see. Make it look like a press kit. For example, you take a folder such as a report folder. On the outside cover print the name of your company printed and a logo or photograph of something related to DNA that won't frighten away the consumer. Simple graphic art such as a map or globe of the world, a prehistoric statue, for example the Willendorf Venus, or some other symbol is appropriate.

Inside, you'd have maps, charts, and locations for the client to look at. Keep the material visual. Include a CD with the DNA sequences if you can. The explanation would show the customer the steps taken to test the DNA.

Keep that visual with charts and graphs. Don't use small print fonts or scientific terminology to any extent so your customer won't feel your report is over his or her head. Instead use illustrations, geographic maps. Put colorful circles on the cities or geographic locations where that person's DNA is found.

Put a bright color or arrow on the possible geographic area of origin for those DNA sequences. Nobody can pinpoint an exact town for certain, but scientists know where certain DNA sequences are found and where they might have sat out the last Ice Age 20,000 years ago, and survived to pass those same DNA sequences on to their direct descendants, that customer of yours who has those sequences.

In the last decade, businesses have opened offering personality profilers. This decade, since the human genome code was cracked and scientists know a lot more about DNA testing for the courtroom, DNA testing businesses have opened to test DNA for information other than who committed a crime or to prove who's innocent. Applications of DNA testing now are used for finding ancient and not-so-ancient ancestry. DNA testing is not only used for paternity and maternity testing, but for tailoring what you eat to your genetic signature. The new field of pharmacogenetics also tests DNA for markers that allow a client to customize medicine to his or her genetic expression.

You may be an entrepreneur with no science background. That's okay as long as your laboratory contacts are scientists. Your most important contact and contract would be with a DNA testing laboratory. Find out who your competitors contract with as far as testing laboratories. For example, Family Tree DNA at the Web site: http://www.familytreedna.com/faq.html#q1 sends its DNA samples to be tested by the DNA testing laboratories at the University of Arizona.

*Bennett Greenspan, President and CEO of* Family Tree DNA founded Family Tree in 1999. Greenspan is an entrepreneur and life-long genealogy enthusiast. He successfully turned his family history and ancestry hobby into a full-time vocation running a DNA testing-for-ancestry company. Together with Max Blankfeld, they founded in 1997 GoCollege.com a website for college-bound students which survived the .COM implosion. Max Blankfeld is Greenspan's Vice President of Operations/Marketing. Before entering the business world, Blankfeld was a journalist. After that, he started and managed several successful ventures in the area of public relations as well as consumer goods both in Brazil and the US. Today, the highly successful Family Tree DNA is America's first genealogy-driven DNA testing service.

At the University of Arizona, top DNA research scientists such as geneticist, Mike Hammer, PhD, population geneticist Bruce Walsh, PhD, geneticist Max F. Rothschild, molecular anthropologist, Theodore G. Schurr, and lab manager, Matthew Kaplan along with the rest of the DNA testing team do the testing and analysis. So it's important if you want to open your own DNA for ancestry testing company to contract with a reputable laboratory to do the testing. Find out whether the lab you're going to be dealing with will answer a client's questions in case of problems with a test that might require re-testing.

Clients will come to you to answer questions rather than go to the busy laboratory. Most laboratories are either part of a university, a medical school, or are independent DNA testing laboratories run by scientists and their technicians and technologists.

Your business will have a very different focus if you're only dealing with genealogy buffs testing their DNA for ancestry than would a business testing DNA for genetic risk markers in order to tailor a special diet or foods to someone's genetic risk markers.

For that more specialized business, you'd have to partner with a nutritionist, scientist, or physician trained in customizing diets to genetic signatures. Many independent laboratories do test genes for the purpose of tailoring diets to genes. The new field is called nutrigenomics.

Check out the various Web sites devoted to nutrigenomics if you're interested in this type of DNA testing business. For example, there is Alpha-Genetics at http://www.Alpha-Genics.com.

According to Dr. Fredric D. Abramson, PhD, S.M., President and CEO of AlphaGenics, Inc., "The key to using diet to manage genes and health lies in managing gene expression (which we call the Expressitype). Knowing your genotype merely tells you a starting point. Genotype is like knowing where the entrance ramps to an interstate can be found.

They are important to know, but tell you absolutely nothing about what direction to travel or how the journey will go. That is why Expressitype must be the focus." You can contact AlphaGenics, Inc. at: http://www.Alpha-Genics.com or write to: Maryland Technology Incubator, 9700 Great Seneca Highway, Rockville, MD 20850.

Why open any kind of a DNA testing business? It's because the entrepreneur is at the forefront of a revolution in our concept of ancestry, diet, and medicines. Genes are tested to reveal how your body metabolizes medicine as well as food, and genes are tested for ancient ancestry or recent relationships such as paternity. Genes are tested for courtroom evidence.

So you have the choice of opening a DNA testing service focusing on diet, ancestry, skin care product matches, or medicine. You can have scientists contract with you to test genes for risk or relationships. Some companies claim to test DNA in order to determine whether the skin care products are right for your genetic signature. It goes beyond the old allergy tests of the eighties.

"Each of us is a unique organism, and for the first time in human history, genetic research is confirming that one diet is not optimum for everyone," says Abramson. Because your genes differ from someone else's, you process food and supplements in a unique way. Your ancestry is unique also.

Do you want to open a business that tunes nutrition to meet the optimum health needs of each person? If so, you need to contract with scientists to do the testing.

If you have no science background, it would be an easier first step to open a business that tests DNA only for ancestry and contract with university laboratories who know about genes and ancestry.

Your client would receive a report on only the ancestry. This means the maternal and/or paternal sequences. For a woman it's the mtDNA that's tested. You're testing the maternal lineages. It's ancient and goes back thousands of years. For the man, you can have a lab test the Y-chromosome, the paternal lineages and the mtDNA, the maternal lineages.

What you supply your clients with is a printout report and explanation of the individual's sequences and mtDNA group called the haplogroup and/or the Y-chromosome ancestral genetic markers.

For a male, you can test the Y-chromosome and provide those markers, usually 25 markers and the mtDNA. For a woman, you can only test the mtDNA, the maternal line for haplogroup letter and what is called the HVS-1 and HVS-2 sequences. These sequences show the maternal lineages back thousands of years. To get started, look at the Web sites and databases of all the companies that test for ancestry using DNA.

What most of the DNA testing entrepreneurs have in common is that they can do business online. People order the DNA testing kit online. The companies send out a DNA testing kit. The client sends back DNA to a lab to be tested.

The process does not involve any blood drawing to test for ancestry. Then the company sends a report directly to the customer about what the DNA test revealed solely in regard to ancient ancestry—maternal or paternal lines.

Reports include the possible geographic location where the DNA sequences originated. Customers usually want to see the name of an actual town, even though towns didn't exist 10,000 years ago when the sequences might have arisen.

The whole genome is not tested, only the few ancestral markers, usually 500 base pairs of genes. Testing DNA for ancestry does not have anything to do with testing genes for health risks because only certain genes are tested—genes related to ancestry. And all the testing is done at a laboratory, not at your online business.

If you're interested in a career in genetics counseling and wish to pursue a graduate degree in genetics counseling, that's another career route. For information, contact The American Board of Genetic Counseling. Sometimes social workers with some coursework in biology take a graduate degree in genetic counseling since it combines counseling skills with training in genetics and in interpreting genetics tests for your clients.

### The American Board of Genetic Counseling.

9650 Rockville Pike
Bethesda, MD 20814-3998
Phone: (301) 571-1825
FAX: (301) 571-1895
http://www.abgc.net/

Below is a list of several DNA-testing companies. Some of these companies test DNA only for ancestry. Other companies listed below test genes for personalized medicine and nutrigenomics, and some companies test for nutrigenomics, pharmacogenetics, and ancestry.

You'll also find several companies listed that only test the DNA of animals. So you have a choice of testing DNA for a variety of purposes, for testing human DNA only, or for testing animal DNA. And the applications for testing genetic signatures are growing, since this science is still in its infancy in regard to applications of genetic and genomic testing.

Roots for Real
http://www.rootsforreal.com
address: PO Box 43708
London W14 8WG UK

Family Tree DNA—Genealogy by Genetics, Ltd.
World Headquarters
1919 North Loop West, Suite 110 Houston, Texas 77008, USA
Phone: (713) 868-1438 | Fax: (713) 868-4584
info@FamilyTreeDNA.com
http://www.familytreedna.com/

Oxford Ancestors
Oxford Ancestors, London,
http://www.oxfordancestors.com/

AncestrybyDNA, DNAPrint genomics, Inc.
900 Cocoanut Ave, Sarasota, FL 34236. USA
Tel: 941-366-3400 Fax: 941-952-9770 Web site:
http://www.ancestrybydna.com/

GeneTree DNA Testing Center
2495 South West Temple
Salt Lake City, UT 84115
Toll Free: (888) 404-GENE
Phone: (801) 461-9757
Fax: (801) 461-9761, http://www.genetree.com/

Trace Genetics LLC
P.O. Box 2010
Davis, California 95617
info@tracegenetics.com
http://www.tracegenetics.com/aboutus.html

## Predictive Genomics for Personalized Medicine including Nutrigenomics

AlphaGenics Inc.
9700 Great Seneca Highway
Rockville, Maryland 20850
Email: info@alpha-genics.com
http://www.alpha-genics.com/index.php

Genovations ™
Great Smokies Diagnostic Laboratory/Genovations™
63 Zillicoa Street
Asheville, NC 28801 USA
http://www.genovations.com/

Centre for Human Nutrigenomics
http://www.nutrigenomics.nl/
According to its Web site, "The Centre for Human NutriGenomics aims at establishing an international centre of expertise combining excellent pre-competitive research and high quality (post)graduate training on the interface of genomics, nutrition and human health."

Nutrigenomics Links: http://nutrigene.4t.com/nutrigen.htm

## Veterinary DNA Testing

Veterinary Genetics Laboratory
University of California, Davis
One Shields Avenue
Davis, CA 95616-8744
http://www.vgl.ucdavis.edu/

According to their Web site: "The Veterinary Genetics Laboratory is internationally recognized for its expertise in parentage verification and genetic diagnostics for animals. VGL has provided services to breed registries, practitioners, individual owners and breeders since 1955." The Veterinary Genetics Laboratory performs contracted DNA testing.

Alpaca/Llama
Beefalo

Cat
Cattle
Dog
Elk
Goat
Horse
Sheep

DNA Testing of Dogs and Horses:
VetGen, 3728 Plaza Drive, Suite 1, Ann Arbor, Michigan, 48108 USA
http://www.vetgen.com/

*       *       *

## Ethnic Genealogy Web Sites:

Acadian/Cajun: & French Canadian: http://www.acadian.org/tidbits.html

African-American: http://www.cyndislist.com/african.htm

African Royalty Genealogy: http://www.uq.net.au/~zzhsoszy/

Albanian Research List: http://feefhs.org/al/alrl.html

Armenian Genealogical Society: http://feefhs.org/am/frg-amgs.html

Asia and the Pacific: http://www.cyndislist.com/asia.htm

Austria-Hungary Empire: http://feefhs.org/ah/indexah.html

Baltic-Russian Information Center: http://feefhs.org/blitz/frgblitz.html

Belarusian—Association of the Belarusian Nobility:
http://feefhs.org/by/frg-zbs.html

Bukovina Genealogy: http://feefhs.org/bukovina/bukovina.html

Carpatho-Rusyn Knowledge Base: http://feefhs.org/rusyn/frg-crkb.html

Chinese Genealogy: http://www.chineseroots.com.

Croatia Genealogy Cross Index: http://feefhs.org/cro/indexcro.html

Czechoslovak Genealogical Society Int'l, Inc.:
http://feefhs.org/czs/cgsi/frg-cgsi.html

Eastern Europe: http://www.cyndislist.com/easteuro.htm

Eastern European Genealogical Society, Inc.: http://feefhs.org/ca/frg-eegs.html

Eastern Europe Ethnic, Religious, and National Index with Home Pages includes
the FEEFHS Resource Guide that lists organizations associated with FEEFHS

from 14 Countries. It also includes Finnish and Armenian genealogy resources: http://feefhs.org/ethnic.html

Ethnic, Religious, and National Index 14 countries: http://feefhs.org/ethnic.html

Finnish Genealogy Group: http://feefhs.org/misc/frgfinmn.html

Galicia Jewish SIG: http://feefhs.org/jsig/frg-gsig.html

German Genealogical Digest: http://feefhs.org/pub/frg-ggdp.html

Greek Genealogy Sources on the Internet: http://www-personal.umich.edu/~cgaunt/greece.html

Genealogy Societies Online List: http://www.daddezio.com/catalog/grkndx04.html

German Research Association: http://feefhs.org/gra/frg-gra.html

Greek Genealogy (Hellenes-Diaspora Greek Genealogy): http://www.geocities.com/SouthBeach/Cove/4537/

Greek Genealogy Home Page: http://www.daddezio.com/grekgen.html

Greek Genealogy Articles: http://www.daddezio.com/catalog/grkndx01.html

India Genealogy: http://genforum.genealogy.com/india/

India Family Histories: http://www.mycinnamontoast.com/perl/results.cgi?region=79&sort=n

India-Anglo-Indian/Europeans in India genealogy: http://members.ozemail.com.au/~clday/

Irish Travellers: http://www.pitt.edu/~alkst3/Traveller.html

Japanese Genealogy: http://www.rootsweb.com/~jpnwgw/

Jewish Genealogy: http://www.jewishgen.org/infofiles/

Latvian Jewish Genealogy Page: http://feefhs.org/jsig/frg-lsig.html

Lebanese Genealogy: http://www.rootsweb.com/~lbnwgw/

Lithuanian American Genealogy Society: http://feefhs.org/frg-lags.html

Melungeon: http://www.geocities.com/Paris/5121/melungeon.htm

Mennonite Heritage Center: http://feefhs.org/men/frg-mhc.html

Middle East Genealogy: http://www.rootsweb.com/~mdeastgw/index.html

Middle East Genealogy by country: http://www.rootsweb.com/~mdeastgw/index.html#country

Native American: http://www.cyndislist.com/native.htm

Polish Genealogical Society of America: http://feefhs.org/pol/frg-pgsa.html

Quebec and Francophone: http://www.francogene.com/quebec/amerin.html

Romanian American Heritage Center: http://feefhs.org/ro/frg-rahc.html

Slovak World: http://feefhs.org/slovak/frg-sw.html

Slavs, South: Cultural Society: http://feefhs.org/frg-csss.html

Syrian and Lebanese Genealogy: http://www.genealogytoday.com/family/syrian/

Syria Genealogy: http://www.rootsweb.com/~syrwgw/

Tibetan Genealogy:
http://www.distantcousin.com/Links/Ethnic/China/Tibetan.html

Turkish Genealogy Discussion Group:
http://www.turkey.com/forums/forumdisplay.php3?forumid=18

Ukrainian Genealogical and Historical Society of Canada:
http://feefhs.org/ca/frgughsc.html

Unique Peoples: http://www.cyndislist.com/peoples.htm Note: The Unique People's list includes: Black Dutch, Doukhobors, Gypsy, Romani, Romany & Travellers, Melungeons, Metis, Miscellaneous, and Wends/Sorbs

## Use Corel's WordPerfect Office Suite 12 or Beyond to Launch Or Pre-Sell Your Book to the Media Before You Find A Publisher or Agent.

Begin by using your Corel Graphics Suite 12 or beyond (whatever comes next) to create a senior citizen, parenting, or teen hub (in a brochure) with images and text. Send your brochure to the Web. Look at any teen hub, such as Goosehead. There's still room for other shows like Goosehead, and one could feature your unpublished writing. Or you could create a similar venture yourself online. You could create content for shows such as Goosehead.

The teen hub came about when a 14-year old girl named Ashley Power with her personal Web site caught the attention of Richard Dreyfuss. He made a deal to create content for Goosehead. How did such publicity come to a 14-year old's personal Web site?

Thousands of girls from 11 to 15 daily have personal Web sites and need content. One day actor Richard Dreyfuss's niece appeared in a Goosehead video series. It's quite a leap and rare that the niece of an actor appears in a video series that springs out of a 14-year old girl's Web site. Such rarity is what makes for fame. Destiny? Well, Dreyfuss got in touch with Power and made a deal to create at least two interactive episodes to Goosehead.

Look at the site yourself, and decide what about it made it ripe for moving from a 14-year old girl's personal Web site into a video series that caught the eye of a star who writes content for interactive Web.

The episodes, by the way, are called Webisodes. Actually, the technical term is multicasting content as opposed to multimedia that's not always online. Before you test the waters, look at the following sites that use stars to plug products they like.

Then think of ways how you can plug your unpublished writing by plugging a product you like and that a star also likes. Look at www.gooshead.com, www.babystyle.com, www.voxxy.com, www.sightsound.com, www.shockwave.com, www.generationa.com.

Is there anything similar you can do with your sites to produce content or plug a product you like? Use your unpublished writing to move your content, be your content, plug your content, or plug someone else's product you use and enjoy. That's one other way to launch your unpublished books, booklets, scripts, plays, stories, poems, lyrics, content, or learning material.

Scripts, books, and stories that are unpublished can still find a market on the Web if they are customized to the tastes of those who produce such works. If you have ambition and drive, you could aim to producing your own unpublished direct-to-Web material, called entertainment content.

It doesn't have to be fiction. It could be learning materials or documentaries. If you don't want to compete with the entertainment industry, there are audiences who want how-to films or videos that were never videos in the first place, but produced direct-to-Web with good multimedia authoring software such as Director and others.

So keep in mind that you can let your unpublished writing plug any product you like or a star likes and do it online and on TV. If you're into performing arts, start a Web site for teenagers or any other age group.

You can make yourself or anyone else, even a star, spokesperson. The trick is to produce and star in 12–26 half-hour shows aimed at a specific audience, such as teenagers, where you can use your unpublished book to plug the products advertised on the teen magazine Web and/or cable TV show.

You get visibility, publicity, and market your work all at once. If you go for the teen market, produce shows for a Web site, where you'll get to talk honestly with teens about issues they're interested in. Shows can focus in on niche audiences that need Web sites or cable TV teen magazine shows only for them, such as girls from 11–17.

There's one site www.voxxy.com that does just that in new ways. So the point is that if you have a lot of unpublished writing, you want to sell it by getting the chance to have all the input you want at Web sites that draw in the stars of TV looking for shows to produce or be spokesperson for. You want the stars to endorse your writing as they endorse products they enjoy.

The idea of plugging products you like by using your unpublished books and scripts is a form of packaging your books or booklets with products going to be bought. Before the Internet, you'd approach a warehouse or manufacturer and ask that your book be packaged with the products being shipped as a way to give customers a free instructional manual on a product or a sideline, like a cookbook on how to cook with wines or sauces being shipped with packaged wines or sauces.

Now, you do similarly on a Web site, called a Web venture. If you write about baby care, target a Web site for this subject. Try sites such as www.babystyle.com if you're writing books or booklets about baby wear, décor, and care.

It's all about style and babies. Or start your own site focusing on baby style, elder style, teen style, or any other group from men to teenage girls. Women are increasingly on the Web, so you might want a new angle on women's interests, such as genetic counseling, nutrition, customizing diets according to your DNA analysis, romantic fiction, suspense, or cat characters in novels.

Before you get too narrow, pick the audience for the widest possible number of visits to your site. You need to research your markets to find out what people in different targeted groups really want to spend their valuable time visiting.

Find a way to endorse a product or get an important person to endorse a product that will include your unpublished book along with the product being endorsed as a gift or giveaway or additional benefit and advantage to the buyer. Use your writing to plug someone else's products.

If you have an unpublished romance novel, personalize it with the name of the happy couple and package it along with the wedding gifts ordered. Or leave a personalized novel in guest rooms of hotels with the name of the guests, if they order it. Honeymooners might, or it might be of interest to those planning bridal or baby showers, anniversary cruises, or office parties.

The quickest way to launch your book is to stage an around the world online launch party (when most media people are available) inviting the specialty and general press, publishers, agents, entertainment attorneys, producers, directors, book talent managers, book packagers, famous writers, newspaper reporters and columnists from TV as well as print media, small press publishers, book sellers, event planners for booksellers events overseas and nationally, and those who come to book sales parties in people's homes as well as software, book and video distributors to meet you for a conference online where you'll have a chat and put up a presentation with sound, text, and video clips or visuals all about your unpublished book or script.

Did you see the pre release publicity the Harry Potter books received, even coverage on the cover of Newsweek? What can you do for your unpublished book to create spin that will add to your credibility as well as visibility in the media all over the world?

It all starts with a storyboard and a press kit that reveals your main character's measured change, transformation, or growth, or if your book's nonfiction, how much everyone needs to know the information you're about to tell. It's not whom you know, but whom you tell—and how you tell it that brings people together.

## How Do You Make A Storyboard?

Storyboards can help launch your unpublished book if you use them as a kind of mind map that uses the right hemisphere of the brain to express visually with thumbnail sketches and dialogue bubbles what goes into a novel or script.

If you write your story as a play first and flesh out the dialogue into a novel, it will flow easier when based on a storyboard. You can move to a springboard, where you can bounce the story off of the springboard's role as a summary or synopses of significant events and turning points in your book or script.

A springboard runs up to 15 pages long. A story board can go the length of the book summarizing the highlights in half that number of pages. A synopsis runs about one or two pages, and a high concept pitch is one sentence that tells your whole story such as Star Trek is Wagon Train in space.

What's a storyboard? Storyboards are pages of panel cartoon-like visual images of how a chapter or scene looks visually before the dialogue is spoken. Draw in thumbnail sketches your storyboard for each scene of your novel, autobiography, or script as you write it or adapt it from a novel, news clipping, or story.

To pre sell your unpublished book to the media or publishers, write the significant events, turning points, or highlights of your confrontation where two characters with opposite personalities enter into conflict for the last time.

The battle scene is the major test that results in a major change both inside two characters with opposite personalities so each opponent can reach the goal and end the story. This is what you hand to the press and to publishers, agents, or producers. You're highlighting and summarizing the significant events of your book.

1. Hold a mid-night launch party for your life story or other book.

2. Hold a noon launch party for readers who can't drive or go out at night, and have the location on a bus line.

3. Hold a weekend launch party at a department or discount store such as Wal-Mart or any similar store. Or combine with any store's grand opening party.

4. Hold a launch party in a school cafeteria, library, gym, yard, or auditorium for the appropriate age group. Combine launch party with a lecture to elementary or high school classes. Or if more appropriate, to special interest groups and clubs, professional associations, or women's clubs and organizations or related societies.

5. Hold a launch party at a college campus or rent a room or auditorium or space on the lawn.

6. Hold a launch party in a senior citizens apartment complex, recreational center, adult education center, hospital gift shop, or nursing home.

7. Hold a launch party in a place where you can set up an international or national day so that everyone, especially children, if your book is appropriate, can read your book on the same day, in case they do order it. Have all the children across the nation experience Your Life Story or Your Book on the same day.

8. Hold a launch party in a church recreation hall, park, museum, library, art gallery, zoo, space theater, or social center.

9. Hold a launch party in a mall or on the lawn of a public park or skating rink on a Sunday or at a sports center or field.

10. Hold a launch party on a cruise ship before it sails or in a bus or train station or airport.

Put up a temporary kiosk for your launch party. Or get permission and a permit to launch your book near or in front of a supermarket or convention center or a hotel lobby.

Use cruises and travel situations to launch your party. Or charter a flight and launch it in transit to help passengers pass the time. Cruise ships are you best bet.

Ask newspaper reporters from national press associations and public relations associations to cover your book or life story in their articles on lifestyle or business subjects or whatever the subject of your book covers. Societies of professional journalists have monthly meetings. Ask to have your launch party at one of their meetings or invite the whole organization to your meeting.

Gather other writers of similar books and life stories into a pool of vendors and sell booths or tables in a large hall, Masonic center, or other meeting place, like an association of Realtor's Hall, or building you can rent. Have all the writers self-publish their books or photocopy with cardstock cover and illustration or photo and comb binding. Print on demand.

Have numerous copies of books on tables. A group of 10 or 20 writers can have a group launch party and invite the press or sponsor a press club meeting, perhaps on board a docked yacht that's rented for the day or in a hotel or university rented room or meeting hall. Books can be printed on demand and given as press copies to reporters.

Invite entertainment and copyright attorneys, agents, publishers, editors, the media, and writers, also the potential readers of your book such as children and parents or business people. Have your launch party at a convention or conference on a related theme, such as a conference of small press publishers or a book buyer's convention or annual meeting in the US or abroad. Or take a group of writers on a cruise and present books to the press.

You can go free if you gather enough paying people to take the tour with you. Have stationery printed with a logo or slogan. Print the letterhead with enlarged slogan or logo onto a supply of two-pocket folders.

Print a scriptwriting logo onto adhesive labels. Stick the labels onto the cover of the folders. The multi-colored two-pocket folders are available in any office supply outlet.

Create a brochure, preferably in color. Include the brochure in the press kit.

The brochure could list a writer's services and credentials or credits. If there are no past credits, print all the services provided such as quality circles for writers, individual instruction, seminars, event planning for communications professionals, freelance technical writing, manual writing, corporate scriptwriting, desktop publishing, word processing, editing, tutoring, instructional courseware design, children's writing instruction, corporate scriptwriting, English as a second language writing instruction, or fiction written for adults with 2nd grade reading ability, science journalism, writer's speakers bureau, art, publicity writing, or any other type of writing services offered.

When Your Best Writing Still Isn't Selling, Here Are The Steps To Take: Use your WordPerfect Office Suite for Cover and Follow-Up Letters. The write a fast-selling 98-page pop-culture booklet for store impulse counters.

**Winning Strategies and Guerilla Tactics To Promote, Publish, and Sell Your Writing Fast:**

Here's how to write and sell a fast-selling paperback 98-page (when published) pamphlet or booklet, the kind you see on supermarket impulse racks at the check stand. They can sell quite a number of copies, or you can sell them by mail order or online from your Web site.

Start by writing about twice the number of pages that will be published. For a 98-page booklet, about 196 double spaced typed pages produces, usually a single-spaced booklet with double spaces and headlines between the sections. You may come out with having to write less than 196 pages, it depends upon the font and size of the booklet. However, here are the dimensions you'll need.

The size of the booklet may either be six inches wide by nine inches in length or five and a half inches wide by 8 inches or 8 1/2 inches in length.

Take your choice. The difference is that trade paperbacks of 6 by 9 inches fit on supermarket impulse racks at checkout counters, whereas the mass market paperbacks you see in supermarkets and book stores in the back areas on special 5 by 8 book-size racks are standard for novels in the mass paperback market.

Let's say you choose the 6 by 9 size, which is the best fit for the impulse check out stand supermarket size. It will also fit into gift shops and specialty store racks. You'll have a soft, glossy cover with your price, usually $2.99 printed on the upper right hand corner of the book cover.

The title will be placed in the middle of the book cover toward the upper half. It will be centered and have a two-word to five-word title that speaks volumes about what's in your little paper book.

In the middle of the cover, explain in one short sentence in smaller font, about 24 point what your book shows people how to do. It must be a how-to book such as how to find and keep a soul-mate, or some other how-to theme.

Below the explanation is the author's name: by, Joe John or whatever name you want on the cover. Inside the cover on the left hand side you print the name of your publishing company. Assuming you're publishing the booklet yourself, put an intelligent-sounding two-word name for your publishing company such as Behavioral Digests and trade mark your publishing firm, even if it's only you at home.

Then under than you can put a longer publishing company name, just in case you want to publish other items besides these little paperback booklets.

Put something light Published by International Palm-sized Books, Inc., and your address. You can incorporate your publishing company. Use an office address or a PO Box number, not your home address. You don't want people showing up on the front steps.

Under that put: Copyright, the year, by, your publishing company, address and e-mail address. Leave out your home phone. You can add a disclaimer in small font at the bottom that "Reproduction in whole or part of any (your publishing company's name) without written authorization is prohibited. The add at the bottom, "printed in the USA" or wherever you send the booklet to be printed. I understand printing prices in Singapore are great, so I hear from greeting card publishers nowadays.

On your first page's right hand side, print the name of the book centered up close to the top of the page, leaving a 2 inch margin from the top. Put in a small clip art illustration or your own art, and then a line and a by (author's name) at the bottom, leaving another 2 inch margin from the bottom.

The left hand side of the first page can have an illustration centered. On the right hand side put your table of contents. Label it Contents.

Divide your booklet into six small chapters and list them. Let's say your book is on how to find a rich mate. Label it with a title, such as why am I single? Then have a second chapter on your cure-all for loneliness.

A third chapter on raising your feeling of importance, a fourth chapter on how to appreciate being by yourself in various settings, a fifth chapter on how to find your soul mate and where to look, and a last or sixth chapter on how to keep your mate once you found him or her.

Mostly women will buy this book on impulse, but if the book is labeled, how to pick up girls, of course it will attract guys or anyone who wants to meet girls.

The left hand side of your table of contents page should have artwork on it centered. Then on page 7, a right-hand side page, your first chapter begins with the title, self-explanatory and short, usually asking a question which you will answer in your first chapter.

Define your question and answer it. Keep each chapter four printed pages, which is eight double spaced type written pages. When made single-spaced, each chapter runs to about four printed pages each.

Then start your second chapter on page eleven. Break your booklet up into segments or chunks. The printing will be singled spaced with double spaces between each section or segment heading that tells the reader how to solve a problem or fill a need.

The problem could be technical or personal, business-oriented or relationship-oriented, health-directed, or about healing and nutrition, parenting, or any subject likely to land on a supermarket check out counter's impulse rack.

After every 14 or 14 chapters, usually 13 to 15 chapters, you'll need a segment or section break with a new title, perhaps outline your case histories, success stories, anecdotes, interviews, or using someone as an example.

Don't use real names unless you have signed permission letters and can footnote that at the end of each chapter in a list of references that's numbered. For brevity, use a first name only and an initial, usually a fake false name approved by whomever you interview with an asterisk saying the name was changed to preserve privacy.

Use more than one example, usually two or three case histories. You can also use celebrity examples if you can get permission for success stories that run about 13 paragraphs each.

Have sections divided if you can around page 19, 21, 23, and start another chapter heading around page 28. Every two pages should have section breaks with new headings. You might write and publish a booklet on journaling and describe how it's related to a feeling of self-importance or of accepting oneself as "good," or write a technical or business how-to if you're not an expert on relationships.

More women will buy these booklets if they're about relationships. You can focus on instructional booklets on any topic from needlepoint and crafts to how to paint furniture and offer it to do-it-yourself stores, such as the big chain stores that customers frequent to buy do-it yourself materials for home repair and building. Another fast-selling area is travel writing.

This would focus on where to go and how to find specifics from antiques to restaurants and entertainment for various ages, education, visual anthropology, or special needs, such as traveling with multiple disabilities or traveling with one's dog or cat. One person trains his cat to use any toilet so he can take it into motel rooms without a litter box.

Your main focus is on how to do something, build something, solve a problem, make choices, or fill various needs, from quilting to relationships. Most people buy booklets with general titles such as how to keep a mate from leaving or how to save a troubled marriage.

Your six-chapter booklet should take up about 98 pages when printed, so don't make it longer or it won't fit into the small books rack in supermarkets and gift shops. It's easier to mail that way. Break your six chapters into three sections that run about two pages each per section with each chapter about four to six pages in length, but vary the length throughout the booklet.

Distribute it yourself or find a distributor who handles the supermarket impulse checkout counter rack. Or you can use gift shops or mail order. Another way to go is to offer your booklet to the tabloids as they have publishing divisions for these types of little books. They'll take a lot of your profit, so my advice is do everything yourself from writing to selling.

A print run of 1,500 copies would test your markets, but do your market research first to make sure someone would buy your book in large numbers. You might try a test run in a supermarket to see if the booklet moves and whether it competes with the tabloid-published booklets of similar size and length.

Will the tabloids let you compete with them in their supermarket client's racks? If not, you have the small gift shops and the malls. If you want to move the booklet, also offer it on tape or online for the e-publishing download market or on a CD or DVD disk. Look at all the marketing alternatives and give your booklet visibility in place where people gather. Career booklets belong in community college and high school career counseling libraries.

Sixty-six-page pamphlets or booklets that are about 4 inches wide and about 6 inches in length. These booklets fill up quickly with your articles. Don't forget to reduce the number of pages you write that first start out as double-spaced typed pages.

Provide marketing research for corporations or information for advertising and public relations agencies, employment agencies, or college career centers in this format or mystery shopper news if updates aren't required more frequently than annually.

If you're printing up an 8 1/2 by 11 inch page, usually it takes up to twice as much writing to reduce the size in half when you print up single spaced content with a double space between paragraphs and allow for a 16 point type size font for each heading or larger fonts for chapter headings,

## Writing, Publishing, and Selling Your Own Small Booklets or Pamphlets

When you print up small booklets, you'll need much less writing to fill up a whole little booklet. These small booklets are bought by school libraries to fill research folders on a variety of topics that are current issues in the news. If you are marketing to the general public through supermarket racks on impulse shelves near the checkout counter, usually near the checkout person, you'll want to supply each supermarket with your own racks the size of your tiny booklets.

The subjects that sell best are topics that tell the reader how something affects or changes something else. For example, how different foods affect your moods, and subtitle the booklet how people can change their behavior or their lives by adjusting the foods to their moods or any other topic telling readers how to improve themselves with the specific information.

Price your booklets anywhere from $1 to $2. Usually $1.19 in the US and $1.49 in Canada is fine, keeping the price plus tax adding up to an even amount. Find out what the tax would be on your booklets to one person at a checkout counter for the booklet. Then adjust the price so the reader can pay the tax and your price and have it add up to an easy to come up with amount, like $1.20 or $1.50. Calculate your expenses so you can arrive at a price that looks inviting.

Keep your pages around 66. Use an even number of pages. Your cover would have a title and a subtitle explaining what the title can do for the reader, how changing the behavior can change the person's life.

Print your company or publishing name and address on the inside cover in the center. On the first page, label it "Contents" and list you six or seven chapters and the page numbers. At the bottom of the contents page, about two inches up from the bottom of the page have the authors name in small, but easily readable font, such as 10 point Times New Roman or italics.

The left hand side of the contents page should have a disclaimer saying that your book is intended as a reference volume, not a medical manual so you won't be sued for giving medical advice without a license or credentials. Put in there that your booklet doesn't presume to give medical advice.

You really need this in there. Add a "consult your physician before beginning any therapeutic program," to protect yourself from being sued or accused of giving medical advice. You need this disclaimer on any booklet that gives information based on material provided by actual researchers and experts, even if you are using medical articles with simplified English or anything where people are told what to eat to change their health or behavior.

Always put this disclaimer or a similar one into a booklet you write and publish. This is especially true when you interview doctors or read their articles and report what they wrote, even with their written permission, which you always need to have. You don't need this disclaimer of your booklet is about how to knit costumes for animals or how to fix a leaky faucet or repair and antique furniture, but you need it for special diet, food, and nutrition booklets.

Each chapter can run four to 12 pages in this tiny booklet with the chapter divided every few paragraphs into new headings so you break up your booklet in chunks. Try to balance the size of your chapters. Usually four-page chapters work best in this size booklet totaling about 6 or 7 chapters, and total amount of pages being about 66.

Keep your pages an even number. Don't leave blank pages in this size booklet. On your back, glossy cover have a one or two-sentence description of the book centered about one inch down from the top. Put it in a box if you like, and put your bar code below with the price on the back. You'll also have the price on the front cover, your logo in the upper left hand corner of the front cover, the title, subtitle, and any illustration, usually a photo in color of a person working with the items in the book or doing some action that sums up what the book says.

Have the book cover put on with two staples in the spine that are not readily noticeable to the reader. Only the backs of the staples should be seen on the spine, and flat into the crease of the spine of the book so as not to catch on any object. You don't need an ISBN number for this kind of booklet, only a bar code so the scanning machine in the supermarket can scan it. Provide your own racks if ones there belong to other merchants and distributors. Have the price on the front and back cover in addition to the bar code so readers can see the price immediately.

If you write on health topics, keep the English simple, writing at 5th grade level. Keep sentences short and paragraphs short, about two sentences per paragraph. Use Times New Roman 12 point type, nothing smaller, or older people won't want to look unless they have their reading glasses. So keep the font large enough for most people to see at most ages.

You can find distributors who specialize in small pamphlets and booklets, or specialize in supplying college and high school career counseling offices with booklets on each type of career in a group of related careers. Or focus on foods and health or psychology and behavior for self-help.

Inspirational booklets have their own market, but if you want people to pay for your booklets, give them information that's harder to find and is not usually found among the free literature available at community or religious centers. Also try specialty gift stores, home building centers, discount stores, libraries, business, professional, and trade associations, corporations, schools, and employee organizations. Writing on contemporary and controversial issues in the news supplies school libraries with information for student research. For more information on getting bar codes or ISBN numbers for your larger booklets, just click on my other article here on writing 98-page booklets and pamphlets.

Winning Strategies or Guerilla Tactics for Sweet Romance Stories or Novels: Turn them into a 4 inch by 6 inch small, 72-page romance story booklets and sell in supermarkets and gift shops or packaged with other products.

Don't forget those wonderful romance novelettes and stories you have that are shorter than book length. If they are sweet romances, short stories in three parts or "acts," of about 23 pages for each act, totalling around 72 pages or so, you can turn them into 72-page, 4 inch by 6 inch booklets, promote, and sell the little pamphlets at supermarkets. They go in the impulse racks at the checkout counters. Most of these small size mini-racks hold booklets about four inches wide by six inches long. This is the ideal size for romance stories or novelettes.

You'll get about a maximum of 300 words on a page: that's a maximum of 10 or 11 words across a line and about a maximum of 30 lines on a page. For first pages of new sections, and you'll have three sections or "acts," you start about two inches down from the top of the page with the first letter of your beginning sentence capitalized and highlighted in a larger font than the rest of the letters.

You'll need a bar code. You don't need an ISBN number unless you also want to send your booklets to gift shops or put your own racks up to match your customized size in supermarkets if they have room, but the small size that holds the four by six inch booklet is fine. If you plan to sell your booklet by mail order to gift shops in hospitals or to libraries, get the ISBN number as well as the bar code. Here's how to organize your little book of sweet romances:

The cover should be a glossy heavier weight paper that can fold easily enough to fit into a small pocket or purse so people can carry the book easily onto transportation. You can market your book at racks in airports, train, and bus stations or at transit centers in vending machines if you buy the empty ones and place them where you can get permission. Hotel lobbies have racks that could fit your book, but usually you supply your own racks to hotels and convention centers.

Resorts and antique malls also are great places for your little book. Tourist attraction shops in the "old town" sections of cities are great. In fact any place that sells tourist souvenirs make great places to sell your little romances. People staying in hotels and motels can read the little books, and you can offer the same size booklets with adventure stories or romances related to the particular town or resort history.

On the cover have an illustration in color of the couple featured in the romance story, usually a cameo of the couple featured against a pristine background of countryside, or local resort attractions. On the top you can put a ribbon-like title "Your (logo or name) Romance Library" or "Historical Romances of the resort city___" or whatever you want to feature as your own publishing and writing library.

This represents your collection of booklets. You can publish your own writing or those from other romance or historical fiction writers. Travel booklets, auto travel games for kids, or travel romances also can be published in this format.

Usually sweet romances sell better than other genres in this type and size of booklet. People want a sweet romance to escape to and to read at night, especially people traveling on business at hotels. The books will be bought by women and female students of all ages, with the highest demographic being in the 18 to 44 age range and the next highest, 44 to 54 age range.

To help sell your romance against the competition, put in a pet character, usually a cat or kitten or a pair of cats in the story that bring the couple together. Your story can feature a female who works at an animal shelter.

In this way you can bring in a real animal shelter and dedicate your booklet to animal rescue volunteers, which helps move the story. You can also donate a percentage of your income from the booklet to help animal rescue shelters of your choice.

Make sure your story is universal and familiar enough to sell anywhere in the country or even overseas. Your booklet also can be translated into languages if you sell to various countries. Keep your library focused on sweet romance because people want to believe that love conquers all and buy these little stories to relax them and to escape the real world, but the story must be real enough so that it could believably happen to the reader.

Your little booklet will be a tiny version of a magazine. In the romance story, keep it around 72 pages as the best-size and weight for handling, mailing, and reading in one sitting. Most people will buy these as they leave the supermarket to take with them during that long hour or two wait in doctors and dentists offices or while taking a two-hour train ride or while on vacation on the beach or in a hotel or during anytime when waiting is necessary.

# WEEK TWELVE

## Where to Start Your Story

Start your story halfway down page 3 with the title of your little book. You'll find about six paragraphs can fit on one page. In a sweet romance story, don't have chapter headings or a table of contents. Instead of chapter headings, you only have the title page with author's name and dedication "to the_____." Fill in to whomever you dedicate the story.

Use three asterisks (***) at the end of each part or chapter of the story instead of chapter headings. The asterisks represent the breaks in the story when the action changes instead of having chapter headings. Your story can run about an average of 23 to 26 pages before the chapter ends with the three asterisks and new action begins, for example, on page 27. Then run the action on to about page 36 and have three asterisks there.

On page 38 the first sentence starts about two inches down with the first letter of the first sentence in larger and highlighted capital letters than the rest of the text.

Your middle chapter ends about on page 62 with page 63 started with new action about two inches in margin from the top of the page and the first letter of the first sentence in highlighted, larger capital letters. You'll notice that the book or story has three acts or three parts. Each chapter can be of unequal or equal length. It doesn't matter as long as it adds up to a total of about 72 pages. So you see, the sweet romance story has, like a full-length stage play or short cinema film, 72 pages made up of three acts. Each act takes up a third of the booklet or story. You have a beginning, middle, and end. It follows the rules for a romance novel with romantic push and pull tension between the characters.

In the story you bring together an unlikely couple that conquer the push and pull tension of first impressions that don't prove true as you flesh out the second and third act where sweet romance proves love conquers all.

You can build up your own romance library of titles from your own writing or those of other authors. Some authors might want to start a cooperative where they share the cost of publication and distribution, but this is up to you.

You'd do well with only your own stories and publishing your own work. Distribute to supermarkets and gift stores. Then add other sources such as racks in hotels, waiting rooms, airports, hospitals, senior centers, community centers, schools, or doctors and dentists' offices, lawyer's offices, and any place people travel or wait, including tourist gift stores in resort areas and theme parks.

Book stores and libraries or vending machines in rest rooms or on the street near supermarkets are good bets for little books. Romance novelettes should run around 72 pages. Keep them even numbers. On the back cover place a two paragraph review of each character the starring male and female of the couple and tell something about the person in one sentence for each character. Use only two characters on the back cover.

Your third paragraph, a one-sentence statement tells what the story is about in a 15-word sentence that is centered in the middle of the page. Below this three sentence/three paragraph description, put a short statement about your romance library or book, such as "welcome to a cornucopia of sweet romance, where love brings different people together" or love conquers all (this one has been used on Mini-Mags). So use your own original statement, "romance unites all." Pick your own logo. The bar code goes at the bottom of your back cover, usually in the lower left hand corner.

Your own logo image goes at the lower right hand corner. Put your banner and initials centered beneath your "Welcome to the world of sweet romance" or other statement. Use your own statement, not the one Mini-Mags uses. Use them for inspiration only or marketing research.

On your front cover have your banner and logo, an illustration in the center, and your price at the lower left hand corner. Pick your own prices, but don't go over $2.00 or you won't compete with the $1.59 of the current ones. Have your 72-page romance novelettes or stories bound.

Don't use staples in a fiction booklet. That's only for how to booklets or tiny pamphlets on how to change something or improve one's behavior or booklets on food and nutrition or health. So be sure to have a bound booklet for romance that has no staples. Research the booklets in existence and show your printer.

This is one way to find winning strategies or guerilla tactics to salvage your wonderful stories if they are rejected and you know they are really as good as similar stories in print and selling wonderfully. If you have revised your stories and have logical reasons and concrete research and marketing tests showing the content appeals to all audiences and could sell well if published, then a 72-page romance story printed and promoted would cost you far less than publishing a romance novel with no way to distribute it.

Do your research first. Talk to distributors, and find out how to get your small racks into supermarkets or other sources where you can sell them. Try news stands and vending machines or packaging your romance stories with other products as a promotion, even honeymoon packages, lingerie, and mail order products such as gift baskets for bridal showers or at writer's conventions. Happy sales. Happy tales.

## Week Thirteen

**How to Format Your Book Manuscript with Corel WordPerfect Office Suite 12 (and beyond):**

Here's how to format a book manuscript. Use your terrific WordPerfect 12 Office Suite and add images using Corel's Graphic Suite 12, or not to date this book, whatever comes beyond number 12. At the time this book goes to press, the latest version is Office Suite 12 and Graphics Suite 12.

The acquisitions editor of whatever publishing company you'll be using for your own writing will hand your book to a group of readers after spending about 20 seconds getting a first impression. Your book manuscript is read as if it were a resume.

They expect white 20 pound 8.5" X 11x" paper without textures. The acquisitions editor will photocopy your outline, proposal, synopsis, cover letter, and sample chapters or if fiction, completed book when requested.

If the paper weighs more than 20 pounds, it will be hard to photocopy, and thin, onion-skin paper will tear in the automatic photocopying machine. If you're in another country, send a clear photocopy of your work on this type of paper, if possible. Your book, again, is your resume and application for a business partnership or employment and needs to reflect that business mood.

The cover page will contain your book title, the division of the publishing house for which your book is intended, and the number of words and pages. You put your name and address on the cover sheet and the date. After your cover page, insert a blank sheet and put another blank sheet after the last page to protect the last page of your book from creasing and tearing.

My favorite romance of this size is author, Kathleen Dreesen's sweet romance story, "Loving Touch." It runs the standard 72 pages, and the novelette booklet is published by American Media Mini Mags Inc., MicroMags logo. Her booklet is dedicated to the staff and volunteers at We Care Animal Rescue, St. Helena, California.

The characters are fiction. Only their love is real, says the statement on the first page. I highly recommend reading this booklet to get an idea of the size and type of story that sells well.

On the inside of your cover, put your name, business address, and email. Put the date of the copyright and where it was printed, in the USA or elsewhere. Your title page would have the title centered, the author's name beneath it, and any dedication. On the back of your title page, print any information regarding your decision to accept or not accept unsolicited manuscripts from other writers.

Otherwise, you may get everyone sending you their romance stories in hopes you'll publish them. You don't want your mail or email blocked, so print a statement that you'll only take one-page queries if you're interested, or whether you don't want anyone sending you their own stories to publish.

Editors want a standard of one inch margins all around each page, on everything. Leave room for the reader's and editor's notes on top of the page. Your header is standardized at one inch from the top page and a half inch higher than where your text starts. Make sure your header is the same width as the text line.

On this page, you put the title of your book, your name, and the page number on the upper right corner. Use your full or last name (last name is preferred by most editors).

Use the same font throughout, preferably Times New Roman 12 point. Don't send books in any other font as editors are required to convert for typesetting departments to Times New Roman 12. So convert it if it's in Courier, Ariel or another font. Make sure the font is as black as you can get it and the paper is really white, not tan. It has to be photocopied without a shadow.

Most books accepted had more white space and paragraphs under ten lines. Rejected books almost always didn't have these appearances. When mailing your book, put it in a clear plastic bag, the kind you get from the supermarket or meat counter, with no printing on the bag.

The green or red printing comes off with moisture and ruins the book with stains. So no print is placed on the bag. After your book is in the clear plastic (transparent) bag, fold it over so it fits well around the book and put a small bit of transparent tape in the middle. Then put two rubber bands around your manuscript. One rubber band will be at the top and the other at the bottom to hold the plastic bag in place better and to keep pages together.

Don't send a manuscript in a loose-leaf binder and don't put clips on it. Leave off any file folders. Put the manuscript along with a sturdy self-addressed stamped envelope inside a large envelope with book padding. Make sure the return envelope won't tear in shipping and handling when it's returned. Have the correct number of stamps on the envelope.

Also add to this before sealing, a self-addressed stamped post card the editor can return to let you know your book is received. You'd be surprised at the long way this courtesy goes and the effect it has on readers or editors about your attitude to save them the postage of a receipt reply. Print up some business cards and put this into a small envelope with your return card, so you'll look more like a professional writer with a business card.

Have a query letter or cover letter on top of everything so the editor will know what you want done with the book and what it's about, and perhaps a guide to the synopsis. In one paragraph or preferably one sentence, state or pitch what your book is about: "Star Trek is Wagon Train in Space."

Never embarrass an editor by sending a gift or artsy crafty item with a manuscript because everything will be returned after going in the slush pile. Manuscripts must never be faxed. They use up the editor's paper supply and make an awful impression on your attitude and boldness. You want to make an impact of courtesy and business-like manners, an aura of professionalism.

Every time someone faxes a manuscript or synopsis, usually it's rejected and taken as an insult for tying up the fax machine and using up the paper at the other end. So treat your manuscript as if it were your best resume. Show your enthusiasm by a professional, business-like attitude and common courtesy.

## How to Write About Your Most Powerful Source

**Write About Positive Hooks. People Don't Want to Read About Pain All The Time. Nourish People, and Cheer Them Up. Which Sells More— Joy, Nourishment, or Fear? Do People Ever Get Tired of Hope When Offered as Action?**

The reason nourishment books like the "Chicken Soup" series sold so well is because the books bring joy instead of dumping pain on the reader. Dump the pain in therapeutic writing, but in writing you want to publish for a large audience, offer nourishment for the soul, mind, health, and wallet.

People buy more books on the habits of millionaires and efficient people than they buy books surveying the plight of those in poverty or pain, especially when no quick solutions are offered. People want the secrets of healing, love, wealth, and happiness—in short, nourishment from a book, how to enhance creativity, or information on how to build or repair something and how to find inspiration, motivation, joy, and contentment.

Include the press kit when giving presentations, seminars, interviews, radio or T.V. appearances or querying editors, producers, publishers, agents, and entertainment attorneys. Send the press kit to newspaper and magazine editors, television producers, and radio talk show hosts seeking guests from the writing community. Even mystery and suspense novels or true crime accounts have to offer more than violence and justice.

The purpose of a press kit is to inform people that scriptwriting is being done on a full-time basis and assignments are wanted either re-writing other writer's scripts or created fiction or non-fiction video and film scripts for production. Industrial video and the trade magazines are constant users of video scripts for training.

Press kits are included in presentations, pitching, written proposals, sales packets, query letters, and in general correspondence. Marketing and sales for home-based scriptwriters are fields worth writing about in print and in training video script format.

## How Do You Create A Powerful Media Hook?

Every scriptwriter needs an online press kit to pre-sell a script to the video or film market. Most print press kits are discarded by the media without being opened, unless you're well-known. The only way the media will pay attention to a press kit is if it contains a powerful hook. Have one sentence or question that will repeat at the beginning, middle, and end of the press kit. Bring the media to your Web site before you mail out expensive printed material to someone who doesn't contact you and ask for a review copy or press kit of your work.

Use a question hook that makes a busy editor stop and think. Make the question personal and universal. Put on the press kit's cover a hook question that makes the media do some introverted thinking. In large type letters have the question hook read something like, "What's the most powerful resource you have?"

Notice that that hook question is the same as the one you ask of your hero when creating a screenplay, novel, or short story. Another powerful hook question is, "How many times have you sold out on your real dreams and settled for something less?"

This question is also the same as the writer would ask of a hero in creating a novel, story, or screenplay. The hero's individual reactions form the story structure. The editor's reaction creates news coverage in the form of free publicity. Use a personal hook question, not a statement, both on the cover of the folder and inside in the press release. A scriptwriter has to be a professional media strategist, an architect and designer of 'models' on paper that create visibility in the media for the unsold, pre-sold, or in-development script.

Use a hook question in the middle of the press release that reads something like, "If you could perform one act what would it be?" You're exerting your power here, or writing about someone who needs to find power or come out of a powerless situation.

Again, that's the same question the hero in a screenplay or novel would be asked to elicit individual actions. The only reason to create a question hook is to find the largest audience in the shortest time.

A professional-looking press kit publicizes a script, book, or freelance writing business inexpensively. Paid advertising would cost hundreds of dollars for a two-inch display ad in daily newspaper or high-circulation trade journal.

A press kit is an open invitation for the writer to be hired by colleges of extended studies at $50 an hour or 50% of the gross of student's fees to give a one-day seminar on writing. Experience is more important than a degree at such adult education seminars in private schools. This kind of exposure, such as giving seminars for producers and directors on script analysis and consulting leads to better chances to have personal screenplays seen by producers.

Stop using fear as an advertisement to draw people in. There are enough ads on TV that start with a screeching ambulance and a man shouting how he's dying. These ads are broadcast after midnight or late at night so if you fell asleep in front of your TV set, they shock you out of your sweet dream with fearful possible reality scenario to get you to buy their safety products. It doesn't work with older people who may be shocked into a panic attack or worse by the sudden noise of screaming sirens and shouting.

You sell serenity and joy, and stop using fear hooks as they don't work with older or frail people who get sick watching other people getting sick. If you want to sell some product or piece of writing, use positive hooks to bring people to places in life or countryside where a quiet joy offers serenity, like a fountain gently babbling, a scene at the beach calm and joyous, or a gentle garden.

A screenwriter or novelist sells service, not only a script. Describe how the script or videowriting service is used—and end. These strategies also work for nonfiction books or columns. For nonfiction, use an insightful, popular, and commercial short two-word title such as "Robot Cowboys" Or a slightly longer, but snappy, trendy title that tells the whole story of the nonfiction book: "Why Writers Want More Monies and Publishers Want More Funnies." Or "Why Women Want More_____and Men Want More_____"

## What Do Media Professionals Expect To See?

Newspaper and magazine editors, radio and T.V. producers, agents, publicists, entertainment attorneys, directors, actors, film, and video creative directors are used to receiving professionally printed press kits. They only read material sent in an "acceptable format."

An acceptable press kit consists of a double-pocketed file folder, the question hook printed on the cover (not typed on a regular typewriter, but typeset with desktop publishing fonts). Inside the flap pocket is another question hook on the inside cover. In the flap-pocket is a black and white glossy photo of the writer (matte for television producers).

On top of the photo is a four-page press release about what the writer has to offer that needs visibility—and how the information will help the community or readers. A short, one-page press release goes on top of the four-page release. The short press release gives the writer's biography, credits, credentials, and anything else important the writer has done in relation to what the longer press release covers.

News clippings about the writer or the script are put over the short press release. The clippings are cut out, dated, titled, and pasted on a sheet of paper and then photocopied onto a slick, camera-ready white sheet.

Include in the second flap pocket a copy of any article, booklet, book, sample, or tape for media review. This press kit goes to agents as well as media editors and producers.

What does a press kit pitch? Place a two-page pitch release on top of all the other information in the kit tells the media why the script is so extraordinary, so unique and different and who can benefit by seeing it. Include a marketability study of who would be buying the script, book, or tape. The new age video market is on the rise.

On top of every release, place the final cover letter as a courtesy, telling why you want the media to print selected press releases and the photo inside. The cover letter is one page or less in length. The first paragraph of the cover letter contains a premise—of the release. What's important is summarized in one sentence.

Use concrete credentials that can be checked. If the press kit is going to a publisher to sell a book/script package deal, include a chapter breakdown. The titles of the chapters sell the book just as the title of a video script determines its commercial appeal.

Book chapter summaries vary from three paragraphs to under a page for highlights. Tell the media exactly what viewers will be told when they view the script. For script/booklet combinations such as book and audio tape combinations, or video and instructional manual packages, write down the components of the book in a press kit, and send a sample. This technique holds true for self-published and self-produced video/book packages used for instruction or motivation.

The first chapter of a book is like the first scene of a video script. It's the selling chapter. In a press kit designed to sell and outline a book and video package, tell the reader why she needs to read the book and view the video. Include photos or a mock-up copy of the video or book combination.

The fastest way to impress a reader about a video is to have an advertisement or poster with a black background and white print. The print is superimposed over a photo in the background. Viewers will remember that video above one on a white background with black lettering and design.

It's possible to create an infomercial to mail out to potential buyers who might be interested in purchasing a produced video or a published book, but it's expensive. A press kit creating visibility for a video, a script, or a book is more direct. Use one sentence to summarize your book, pamphlet, article, or script's premise.

Marketing researchers often report that readers will respond faster to an article written by a reporter about a person, business, or product than to a paid advertisement placed by the entrepreneur. An article I wrote for a high-circulation paper brought in 600 requests for information when I included my post office box number. The tiny, classified ad I placed in the back of the paper (which was expensive for me) brought no responses.

Visibility influences marketing. Contacts with video software distributors lead to contacts with producers. A commercial title can pre-sell a script. Free publicity and press coverage pulls more weight than small, paid display ads announcing "script for sale." Press coverage is free, and can be obtained by a phone call and a news angle or a press kit.

The market for video scripts is wide and covers fiction and nonfiction. Networking with people in the industry and the press, including the trade press, makes selling a script smoother.

## A Digital Renaissance
## Where Creative Writing Meets E-Publishing

> Writers, your new medium is here…
> You can be among
> the first to branch out into interactive intuitive writing
> on the Web.

Now is the time to start writing for the newest media, whether it's news, education, entertainment, or a hybrid mixture of all of the above. Today's Web provides news and entertainment in cyberspace, as well as education, job training, and college degrees.

### Self Promotion of Your Writing Before and After Publication
### Create Visibility by Plugging Products You Like to be packaged with your books, pamphlets, tapes, or other writing.

If your book is accepted, your expenses will soar. You have to promote your own books online. You'll need to make public appearances also and chat online. Your Web site is your best marketing tool. Editors are never created equal. One person's opinion will always be different from another's about your work.

Keep mailing lists for self-promotion. Ask your publisher to sponsor your mailing, but you supply the addresses. They don't have time or money to gather addresses beyond a few newspapers.

Hang onto fan e-mail and save on disk. Print out, and send to editors in a collection when asked to do so and only then, after you send a query letter asking when they want the fan mail.

Keep all online reviews, such as those at www.amazon.com pertaining to your book. Most fiction nowadays is bought when writers are discovered after having published in major magazines publishing short stories.

Editors then ask them to write novels and expand their stories or come up with new material. Manuscripts are bought through contests, from the winners. Your personal contact with editors can do more for your book than an agent because the publisher is really looking at the published short stories in magazines to recruit a new crop of novelists.

You get in touch with an editor and find out what conferences the editor will attend so you can meet in person and discuss your writing. More books are sold face to face than most other ways.

If you have a day job, don't quit because writers earning twice their salary or more from books are still holding onto their own day jobs. If you've made the best-seller list many times, you still can't quit because your book will be out of print in two years, most likely. The more successful you are, the more publishers will insist that your sales are higher than they were with your first best-selling books.

Readers will write to your editor or publisher demanding that you write faster, and the publisher will write back to you to give the editors faster turn-around time. You will be expected to make each book better than the one before it. You won't be allowed to only write.

Instead, your time will be taken with editing books that need revising and sending proposals and outlines. Your deadlines will grow shorter the more books you write. I had 3 months to finish each book when I had a contract to write five books for Simon & Schuster in 1985. Each book came in within 2 and a half months. I had to work at this full time, and luckily had no day job (and no income) while all this was going on.

It will take many years before your royalties come in. I get $700 in royalties every six months for a book I wrote in 1994 that's now in its second edition, and it's not even a novel. So plan on taking many years out before you see royalties coming in or advances on which you can live.

My advances ranged from $1,600 to $10,000, with the agent taking a chunk for my five-book contract back in 1985. Nowadays, you can negotiate your own contract and ask for what you want. With an agent, that power is taken away from you and put in the agent's hands. Can you do a better job on your own book? Do your research first. Contact the National Writers Union to find out what your rights are before you go with an agent.

You can ask for more free copies if you need them and publicity, because unless you're famous, you won't get much publicity beyond a press release from the average publisher. Think about publishing your own book and creating your own publicity campaign. Make sure your contract doesn't keep you from writing for another publisher.

If it does, find out whether you can write under pen names to increase your income by writing for more than one publisher, especially when books go out of print quickly. Ask how much time you will be given to write the book and do you have a choice. What's your deadline? Then after the book is sent in, how long will it take, that's the turn-around time, until publication?

Four months before publication you need to start your public relations campaign with the editors and publishers magazines, and with the newspapers, when the book is available. Every need changes in the way of genre, each year. You need to be flexible about what you need to write.

The technological world is unfolding in ways that are great for writers. Time Warner, for example, has launched a high-speed Internet service called Road Runner that supports broadband multimedia broadcasts on the Web. The fiber optic cable connection is one-hundred times faster than a residential telephone line and create a new writer's market for online content. The venture combines the technological expertise of Time Warner Cable with the journalistic resources of Time Inc., and the creative talent of Warner Brothers. Other companies— including Hewlett Packard, Motorola, MCI, and Microsoft—have provided supporting technologies and services to help build the new infrastructure for online data transmission.

It's an opportunity for writers to reach a broader market, making money in creative expression, such as writing innovative programming and content development, or designing illustration, video, and other arts. Companies such as Discovery Communications, Inc., a purveyor of cable TV and Web-based entertainment and information, are developing Web video technology that works within the confines of the Internet. Much of the technology originally developed for interactive TV has been repositioned for digital TV. The popular Web programming language *Java* was originally developed by Sun Microsystems, Inc. for the interactive TV market.

Publisher, Knight-Ridder, Inc., is expanding its newspapers into Web sites—a great boon to journalism majors and seasoned writers. Sybase Corporation, a software firm in Mountain View, CA, has revised its multimedia software first developed for interactive TV so that now it can target Web content writing and programming.

According to the *Los Angeles Times* and CNBC TV, employment in movie production and entertainment has surpassed that of aerospace in Los Angeles and Orange Counties. In other areas, more jobs are opening. In a single year, movie production and amusements accounted for 208,900 jobs in the Los Angeles and Orange County areas alone, compared to 121,400 in aerospace. The same year, film and entertainment added 18,800 jobs.

Digital Domain and Mattel Inc. have developed a joint venture using the vast pool of digital artists and entrepreneurs who grew up in the film industry. Today, moving beyond the film industry, digital arts products, services, scripts, and companies combine to form a whole new industry that merges art with technology.

Cinnabar started in 1982 as a scenic design firm and special effects house for film and television. They are also independent consultants for businesses that want entertainment effects in public spaces for retail environments, restaurants, and other non-entertainment places. It is creative energy that shapes new worlds, animated billboards, displays, and business environments. Writers, artists, and technologists now work together to conceive images and design for businesses ranging from fast-food places to playgrounds.

Art has overtaken commerce, and writers are being recruited by the design-based industries and manufacturers of the digital era.

Cultural-products industries are where the money and jobs are today for writers and artists. Creative expressionists can be found working in fields such as entertainment, apparel, architecture, advertising, public relations, furniture design, and movie production as content developers for CD-ROM and Web-based applications. Cultural industries such as video production are growing fastest because of cutting-edge computer technologies and software development.

Industrial artists and writers are creating a newest media industry, a digital renaissance where content and design share center stage.

Special effects in writing, art, film, commercials, music videos, games, theme park attractions, short 3D films, and cable are bringing the Internet and the new media into the home.

Partnerships with news networks, software developers, and cable TV companies are where writers and artists can look for a place to cash in on a future and a fortune. The digital infrastructure has created a future in which the arts and technology will work as a unit and be channeled directly into people's homes.

The old, 1990s *PointCast Network* broadcasted news and information directly to a viewer's computer screen. Information was customized according to each individual's interest and displayed as a SmartScreen[a]. The service is being expanded to provide news for local areas. Today you can customize your scrap-booking, writing, quilting, design, or desktop publishing skills for any occupation, especially the personal historian or genealogist supplier. Use the newest media.

How are businesses using the newest media?

**http://www.pointcast.com**

The online version of the *New York Times*, published by the NYT Electronic Media Company, is available on the Web at no charge. Each issue is the online equivalent of the daily printed edition, with additional links, forums, and features. Don't miss the crossword puzzle!

**http://www.nytimes.com/yr/mo/day/front**

Using the current authoring tools, most interactive writing and programming, called content development, can be transferred to the Internet with little or no modification. Writing Web content is a new market for writers as well as software engineers, artists, and other entertainment, educational, and technological people.

The Web has created a new field for all types of writers and reviewers called *new media marketing*. Bell Atlantic, Nynex Corporation, and Pacific Telesis Group will focus on the Web with an elaborate site for TV fans who can check out reviews of shows and chat. Reviewers of books, movies, and shows can now reach a broader audience by posting their commentaries online. Instead of focusing totally on interactive programming for CD-ROM or Digital Video Disks (DVD), the Web is now the center of attention for creative writers, artists, courseware designers, reviewers, and writers of technical and business related material.

Specialized writers for science and medicine have their Web niche, too. What brings all of them together is that they are helping to build the body of information we call the Web. You may develop an interactive version of your article or book as a promotion to build name recognition and help sell the printed version. Web sites are customer bases in the making. As the site develops, more links may be added to form a mega-Web site linked to industry giants.

Research has shown that the use of interactive multimedia increases learning retention dramatically. On the average, people retain 20% of what they see, 40% of what they see and hear, and 70% of what they see, hear, and do. Those who have been trained to write for TV, radio, or print can easily shift to writing for the Web. The mediums differ, but the required professional writing skills are similar.

## What is a "content creator"?

Those who majored in communications, journalism, creative writing, English, professional and technical writing, scriptwriting, or related subjects will find an abundance of opportunities in online journalism.

A new electronic journalist may be a news reporter by day and a webmaster by night—combining photojournalism with digital photography online.

Job descriptions and titles are becoming electric and eclectic. Webmasters, web-mistresses, cyberhosts, and media jockeys are new occupations that simply did not exist before. Some tasks of these new occupations are to manage Web sites, track information and traffic on the local network server, as well as to establish links to other sites.

Most authoring jobs in the new media require the writer to use HTML (Hypertext Mark-Up Language) or a newer, higher octave now in design. Programmable extensions in *Java* or CGI script may be used to add programmable features to a basic HTML page. The new journalist is a multimedia producer who combines words with hypertext links, formatting each page to interact with other documents, images, and Web sites.

Online journalists are frequently asked to write their pieces in HTML. There are hundreds of sites on the Web to download tutorials. To find them, simply do a search with any search engine. You'll find over 5,000 references to hypertext or HTML tutorials such as "*HTML is Easy as Hell!*" and "*Composing Good HTML.*" You'll find page design and graphics assistance listing recommended file and multimedia formats for Web documents and lists of books about the Internet.

If you search under 'writers' you'll find long lists of information of interest to writers seeking assignments. You'll find information of pertaining to special interest groups, projects, associations, job services and supplies for writers—as well as publishers' guidelines. To find companies that hire writers who can format in HTML, query your search engine on 'freelance', employers', or 'jobs'. I found many job offers for freelance writers who know how to translate their feature articles into HTML and create Web sites with text, graphics, and animation. Online journalists are usually required to have a working knowledge of Web editing tools and multimedia authoring software.

Journalists must now train in more than the "Big Five" computer applications: telecommunications, word processing, graphics, spreadsheets, and databases.

According to Jerry L. Sloan, Professor of Public Relations at E.W. Scripps School of Journalism, "Students today must have a complete command of the computer, Internet and Web to make it in today's world.

It is nearly as much of a requirement as the ability to write well. We are at a dividing line—those who came before didn't have to have it, although it was a plus. Those coming from behind are quickly catching up, and will be completely computer literate, totally comfortable on the Internet and virtually Webmasters on their own."

Computer applications relevant to the field of journalism should be considered a core subject by colleges, universities and writing schools seeking to prepare students for the writer's market of today and tomorrow. The skill level required for general assignment has been raised to a higher octave.

## Who are the new journalists?

The BECA Department at San Francisco State University offers a program in radio and television broadcasting augmented with courses in digital audio production, desktop video production, new communication technologies, and writing for the newest media.

http://www.sfsu.edu/~beca/info/592-1.html

Take note of the strategic alliances developing between telephone, TV, cable, publishing, and software companies. It's collaboration between companies on a level never seen before. For example, Time Warner Entertainment recently became an equity partner in Interactive Digital Solutions, a joint venture with Silicon Graphics, Inc. and AT&T Network Systems. The mission of the company is to provide integrated, multimedia software environments for interactive services. What does that mean?

It means that if you're a writer, it's time to ask your local cable companies about their strategy for the Web. Find out which companies are offering high-speed or satellite Internet services. Whether the connection is by fiber optic cable or digital modem, these new ISPs (Internet Service Providers) will be in need of compelling content to differentiate themselves from the competition.

Tele-Communications, a cable operator, helped start the interactive TV movement several years ago. The company has invested in an online venture called *@Home*. This Englewood, Colorado firm wants to spread the news about high-speed

Internet delivery. In 1996, approximately one third of AmErican homeowners had computers, but only ten percent took advantage of online services. Even so, the Web was well on its way to becoming a mass medium. For non-PC users, the biggest obstacles for going online have been the high cost of computers, the availability of relevant information, and the complexity of the Internet. According to one recent study, seventy-five percent want the Internet to be easy to use and lead them on a pursuit of their personal interests.

With the introduction of WebTV, Internet access has become available to nearly every home in the United States—dramatically changing the profile of the typical Internet user. The latest Nielsen studies, which were based on the PC-using population, showed the typical Internet user to be a male between 25 and 44 years of age, with thirty-four percent college graduates and twenty-five percent with household incomes of $80,000 or more, These statistics will change dramatically as the daytime TV watching consumer audience logs onto the Internet. What kind of online traffic jam this will create is anybody's guess, but one thing is certain—it's serious business where big money is being spent.

17.2 million personal computers with
CD-ROM drives are
currently in U.S. homes;
by 1997, that number is expected to grow to 46.2 million.

—Robertson Stephens

Is the Web ready for professional writers?

At-home demand for online access explodes as American households log onto the information superhighway.

In 1995, an estimated 6.8 million American homes used their PCs to access online services and entertainment. Online access from PCs is projected to grow to 19.9 million households by 2000.

—LINK Resources

## Desktop Publishing and Graphic Design Converges with Web Broadcasting—Creating New Job Descriptions

Q: **How is the convergence of broadcasting and the Web changing the global market?**

A: The coming convergence is the most profound technological change of the 20th century and is also one of the most confusing. Politicians and scholars throughout the world have heralded the emergence of the "Information Superhighway" and the "Global Information Infrastructure" as events that will revolutionize the ways in which we live, play, work, and do business. And yet, even today, few people truly appreciate what these changes mean or how they will affect their lives.

Most of us know this phenomenon has something to do with computers and telecommunications. Many are aware that it involves the Internet and the Web. And quite a few have used some of its first-draft applications, like electronic mail, online shopping, and electronic chat rooms. But the Information Superhighway remains an adjunct to most people's lives, a supplement to traditional ways of doing things, a recreation. Its potential to transform still waits in the wings.

Q: **Will the Internet transform our cities into "smart communities"?**

A: Transform it will. In the mid-nineties, San Diego Mayor, Susan Golding, whose city launched once of the earliest "Smart Community" initiatives, noted that "the planetary equations of wealth and power are tilting more swiftly and profoundly than anyone could have forecast just a few years ago. Those prepared for this titanic shift will become the world's next superpowers. Those that are not may well be condemned to electronic obscurity."

History here is a useful instructor. In the early days of the American West, many once-booming communities became literal ghost towns when their gold or other resources dried up. More than a century later, cities unprepared for the emerging technological changes may suffer a similar fate, becoming "electronic ghost towns" on the virtual frontier, abandoned by corporate and human citizens seeking a more enlightened leadership and a more electronically hospitable environment. If that happens, the urban problems of today—so pressing, even overwhelming to many local leaders—may become very small indeed.

Q:  **Who is driving the technological convergence?**

A:  Techno-visionaries. This technological convergence can be seen in what we'll call "The Three Ms of the New Millennium: the means, the money, and the message." As MIT Lab's Nicholas Negroponte pointed out, "Things that think, will want to link," according to the February 2001 issue of an *Upside* magazine article, "Evangelizing the Internet," by Eriq Gardner.

What is driving these technological changes is something futurists have long referred to as "convergence"—the melding of television, telephony, computers, and the Web into a single global communications network. Even a few months ago, the forecasts of convergence would have struck all but the most fanciful as events destined for another lifetime. But that convergence is no longer the futuristic dreamstuff of technovisionaries. It is here—today. And it will transform our lives as has no political or technological development in the last fifty years.

Q:  **What is the means?**

A:  Since the dawn of convergence-think, the technology of convergence has fallen far short of its dreams. No longer. The first affordable television set-top boxes now have arrived that make it possible for people with no computer experience and little technological sophistication to navigate the Web on an ordinary television set. Internet for the masses is here—today.

Of course, anyone who has used the Web knows that sometimes it seems to take forever to download even simple graphics. But again: no more. Cable modems and other high-speed digital modems are now being marketed that are from 100- to 300-times faster than conventional modems, using the same coaxial cable and copper telephone wires that are already in or near almost every American home.

The expanding network of Internet-capable satellites and fiber-optic cable will boost transmission speeds even higher. The result: real-time, theater-quality video, audio, and virtual reality soon can be delivered to almost every home, business, and institution in America—not over network television or cable TV or VCRs, but by means of the Web. In fact, by the year 2005, MIT's Nicholas Negroponte predicts that more Americans will be on the Web during prime-time than will watch network television.

Q: **Is there money to be made?**

A: Just over a year ago, Netscape Communications, maker of the world's most popular Web browsing software, tendered an initial public offering on the U.S. stock market. Here was a company with no corporate track record, no profit, not even any income. Yet it earned $2 billion in a single day in what at the time was the largest IPO in U.S. history.

Netscape isn't alone. Sony, Time Warner, Fox, Paramount, NBC, Intel, DreamWorks, Viacom, and scores of others are collectively investing billions of dollars into convergence technologies and content—today. Microsoft alone is spending nearly $1.5 billion over the next five years. And that's only the beginning.

Q: **What's the message?**

A: What are the great technological giants doing with all this bandwidth and billions of dollars? A lot of guessing, to judge by their own confessions. Apple founder Steve Jobs recently remarked that "the Web reminds me of the early days of PCs. No one really knows anything." The head of Microsoft's Interactive Division admits: "We don't kid ourselves that we know what's going to happen. If someone told me they did know, I'd say, 'Sign'em up.'"

As a matter of fact, a few smart companies do know. Microsoft, long the world leader in computer software, is "morphing into a media company for the new millennium," in the words of *Wired* magazine, devoting more than a third of its research and development staff to convergence technologies and content.

Way back in early 1996, NBC joined with the computer giant to form the world's first global interactive news network, MSNBC. And dozens of thriving start-ups, from San Diego's DigitalTalkTV and Soular Intentions to Hollywood's "Late Net" with Tim Conway, Jr., to New York's American Cybercast, are getting into the act.

Q: **Will the entertainment industry dominate the Web?**

A: Skylight Entertainment is one of the companies leading the way into the new world of real-time online interactivity. As a developer of entertainment content for the Web, we believe that entertainment will be the application that finally brings the masses to the Web—establishing the cultural foundation for what experts predict will be a $6.5 billion market for online shopping by the turn of the century.

Skylight is working with a number of other companies, including Sony Television Entertainment, Soular Intentions, DigitalTalkTV, and Skylight's own global Internet network, Millennium Worldwide Entertainment Broadcasting Company (MWEB), to create the first-ever entertainment properties wholly integrated with commercial marketing applications and designed exclusively for complementary broadcast over both regular television networks and the Web.

Bio

Kevin Hopkins, president of Skylight Entertainment, served as Director of Technology and Telecommunications for San Diego Mayor Susan Golding. In 1995, he was named "Marketer of the Year" for his innovative use of virtual reality to bring the 1996 Republican National Convention to San Diego.
He has served as executive director of California's "Smart Communities" project, staff director for San Diego's "City of the Future" project, communications adviser to the International Center for Communications at San Diego State University, and technology consultant to AT&T, *Business Week* magazine, *Computerworld* magazine, Ford Motor Company, and Science Adviser to the President and the White House.

Voices from the industry:
Kevin Hopkins, Web Entertainment Producer

# WEEK EIGHTEEN

## Desktop Publishers Online

There are many opportunities for writers to work for online publishers or to become online publishers, producers, or broadcasters themselves. One of the early newspapers that bridged the gap between print and electronic publishing was the *San Jose Mercury News* in California.

That newspaper—in the heart of Silicon Valley—kept pace with the early adopters who were ready for interactive electronic publishing. The *San Jose Mercury News* provides a news forum on America Online as well as a news-clipping service, *NewsHound*.

Many writers today who have been downsized from the print dailies are finding work with the digital news publications. One of the biggest attractions of online journalism is that it often doesn't matter where you're located. Writers for the new media can submit all the news that's fit to e-mail. You're never too far away to write for a digital publication, whether you're telecommuting from home or sitting in a telecenter.

The Web offers the writer unlimited research resources—just a click away—ranging from online publications to entire libraries whose doors are always open. One of many resources is *Computer Mediated Communications*, a magazine that reports about people, events, technology, public policy, culture, practices, research, and applications of computer-mediated communication. It's free and comes to you on the Internet.

The Web is leveling the field of publishing and broadcasting for creative writers and journalists the world over. For many, the Web is the only open channel of communication able to bypass the control of an oppressive government. All writers have—or should have—an equal right to express themselves, whether they are home-based, physically challenged, over the "age of retirement," or just out of college and starting their career. The Web is making us rewrite the rules and rethink employment requirements and opportunities. Let the global writing talent think for itself, question all authority, and deliver verified information in a timely, compelling, and aesthetic manner. That's the whole idea.

Students seek new ways to use technology at NYU's Interactive Telecommunications Program. The program works in collaboration with NYU's Center for the Advancement of Technology (CAT) to develop multimedia technologies and relationships with business and industry.

Where are journalists working online?

http://www.itp.tsoa.nyu.edu

The *Columbia Journalism Review* includes a section called *Cybersources* that's full of online research resources for journalists who want to go fishing with the Net.

http://www.cjr.org

Joint ventures and strategic partnerships between software companies, news organizations, and movie studios are changing the face of the Internet. Some of the largest companies are making serious investments to create a new hybrid online broadcast medium for news and entertainment.

## Broadcast News Ventures

Merrill Brown is the chief journalist in charge of MSNBC Interactive, the Internet side of the ambitious new joint venture between NBC News, a unit of the General Electric Company, and the Microsoft Corporation. The venture went on screen in July 1996. So, what happens when the out-going news media culture collides with the introverted corporate culture of a software developer?

"They love e-mail at Microsoft," David Corvo, an NBC News Vice-President in New York, told the *New York Times*. "We're reporters. We use telephones all the time. We've had to learn more e-mail; they've had to learn more telephone."

Furthermore, Microsoft Network's newsroom is almost free from television sets. News is pulled from wire services for MSN's online service. In contrast, Microsoft visitors to NBC News in Manhattan found computers being used almost exclusively as word processors.

"We talk about customers; they talk about viewers," a Microsoft executive told the *New York Times*. "They talk about content; we talk about journalism," Mr. Corvo said. "It's important to make sure we mean the same thing."

"Part of Merrill's charge," Andrew Lack, president of NBC News, told a reporter from the *New York Times*, "is to raise the bar for the people working on the online side so that their skills and experience and journalistic sensibilities match those on the NBC side."

"Some of the younger people who aren't steeped in journalism may sometimes get cockamamie ideas about it," Mr. Brown told the *New York Times*. "We're working on being very careful about what we put out, and not abusing the fact that we can gather tons of information on the Internet, some of which may have limited value."

An example, he said, was polling data that crops up all over the Internet, and may look intriguing but turn out to be flawed. Still, he said, the cultures over all can be melded.

"Superficially, of course, they are very different cultures, referring to the difference between Microsoft and NBC," Mr. Brown told the *New York Times* in a recent article. "But fundamentally, it's a media-news-information culture we're dealing with. For the interactive side, we've hired people from CBS News, from *U.S. News & World Report*, from *Time*, and from the *Far Eastern Economic Review*."

Mr. Harrington has hired people from print journalism as well as television for MSNBC Cable. The 24-hour news and talk channel uses NBC reporters, as well as some special contributors, and in prime time will have news and interview shows using some of NBC's best-known journalists—Tom Brokaw, Bill Moyers, Jane Pauley, Brian Williams, Katie Couric, Bryant Gumbel and Bob Costas, among them.

Together, the two enterprises have hired about four hundred people. On June 3rd in Fort Lee, about three hundred people reported for work for the first time, in a broad, sunny newsroom where each desk has a Hewlett-Packard computer and tiny RCA television set on top.

"It's a tremendous population explosion within NBC, no question," Mr. Lack said. "And I'll tell you candidly, I've been disappointed in my search within electronic journalism for enough capable colleagues to meet the challenge. I've increasingly turned to reporters who have come through the kind of training you get at a major newspaper."

The publisher will tell you what time period to write about, not what you want to write about, unless your books are selling very well in the time period you choose. Most publishers of fiction want different time periods all from one author, not a stereotype, if you write history and fiction. Fiction writers need to write about what works for the publisher.

The plots and settings for sales are predictable. The publisher will tell you what time periods the best sellers are. If you write a series of books, know that they usually sell pretty well. Books on similar themes sell wonderfully if they are not copycats of best-sellers.

Keep a book as short as the publisher will allow. That way, the reader will buy more of your books. Publishers know this and usually turn down thick manuscripts, unless you're already famous for a certain series or line. If you write love stories, find out what works with the publisher before you even start writing.

What ages does the publisher want? What time periods? Countries? In some books of the seventies, a hero couldn't have red hair because it's considered romantic only in a woman. That's a clue to find out what sells first and what they expect from you in plotting and formulas used or despised by certain houses.

After you write a book, there won't be much rest. If accepted, you'll have a lot of revising to do, perhaps re-writing almost every line of a book that is scheduled to be published by a certain date. Then you'll need to revise the page proofs. As you promote your books just being published, the publisher will require you in your contract for a series to start writing more books and show what you've done.

Even best-selling writers have had second or third novels rejected and felt a tremendous let down when the second book in a series was rejected. Midlist writers who don't sell enough books are kept from getting more books to write. Even a new publisher will ask how many of your old books have sold before giving you a new contract for another book.

This is true when the books related or unrelated to the first book's topic. And it works for nonfiction and fiction writers. If all this seems frightening, keep your day job, get that other graduate degree, keep on writing, and think thrice about publishing and marketing your own books, just in case, so you won't be out of print when you need your book most.

You have an unpublished book or booklet, article, play or script and need media publicity before you launch your material or publish your book, before you find an agent or representative for your book, or before you find a publisher. It's easy as using your unpublished book to plug the products you like on a well-trodden Web site. Just become the spokesperson for a Web site that has wide appeal or start one.

For example, www.generationa.com is a site for people over 50. If you sign on as a spokesperson for any new Web site or create your own and make yourself the spokesperson for it, you'll get visibility in those magazine inserts that come with large daily newspapers around the nation.

Perhaps you have a movie script. Don't let it sit on the shelf, if it has been rejected along with the other 50,000 movie scripts floating around Los Angeles each week, make it into an immersive movie or get a group together to raise funds in order for the group to make an immersive movie. Let the audience control the viewing angle. Watch the immersive movie about a mystery taking place in a nursing home called "The New Arrival" at www.atomfilms.com.

There's also a market for children's immersive movies on the Web. You need to bring together people with similar interests to form a group that makes immersive movies for the Web or raises funds to do so.

Have you sent your script yet to a firm that makes immersive movies? They're on the Web if you can research them. Anyway, at least go to the site www.atomfilm.com and watch their immersive movie. Could you envision your script made into an immersive movie? Are you moving, yet? If no action is happening, make your own immersive movie or get graduate students at film schools to help you. Try schools of new media studies that spring out of journalism and film departments.

You don't have to be a celebrity to sign on as the spokesperson for a Web site, all you do is ask the person who created the Web site whether it's okay for you to be spokesperson, or start your own site about a topic in which a lot of people would be interested. In the case of "Generation A," it's for people over age 50. You can choose something of wide interest that fits your writing style or content areas.

Selling an unpublished book will reach a larger audience if you target television, films, and video, but it's slower. Reaching the Web first as a stepping stone to reaching TV, works twice as fast to get you from the Web to daily newspapers and then to TV, radio, video, and finally film. Another doorway opens if you have your own camera and film, even on a small documentary filler type basis.

Contact emerging stars and starlets who want publicity. They can help you use your unpublished books or scripts to plug the products they like, too. Find a medium that reaches the audience you want, the young, the older, the hip, the well-educated, or any other group you need to reach.

Get in touch with directors who produce animation for Web sites. For example, Tim Burton is a producer working on animation for www.shockwave.com. You might find out if your script or book has a market or could use the medium of shockwave. In other words, turn your writing into a desktop movie using the software of shockwave or related products such as Director.

Get in touch with producers and send them your press kit or at least ask whether their might be any interest to link your subject matter interest with what they might be interested in doing in the future or present. It never hurts to ask for an informational interview, even by email or a good cover letter.

Direct-to-Web releases are growing in popularity. For example, enjoy the film, "Quantum Project." It's available on SightSound.com. What's important is that the film is a direct-to-Web release. Instead of being direct-to-video first and then to Web, it completely passes over the direct-to-video phase and goes right into direct-to-Web.

You might try to make your unpublished scripts go direct-to-Web too, or let producers know you have material available. It doesn't hurt to send your resume to the many companies such as SightSound.com or similar ones that produce direct-to-Web films.

## Who Are the Desktop Publishers and Graphic Designers Going Beyond Scrap Booking to Create Personal History Multi-Media Keepsake Albums?

The *New York Times* article reported that "the majority of newcomers are young, in part because they can be paid lower salaries and in part because younger people tend to have more computer knowledge."

"But the primary criteria," Mr. Harrington told the *Times*, "were journalistic skills and interests, and the ability to work together. These are people who want to do news—not entertainment programs, not sports, not talk shows, not television in general, but news."

All new staff members are employees of NBC News, not MSNBC specifically. "This is NBC News on cable, not some parallel universe," Mr. Corvo said.

So, where in this convergence of big business and technology is your next career move? Perhaps one of the most important questions to ask is how will you fit into the group as a writer.

If you're an introverted technical writer, will you be able to make the shift to a bustling newsroom or entertainment atmosphere? Or if you're a journalist—will you fit into the corporate culture of a software developer as a content writer creating interactive instructional material for employee training? Will you be happier writing news and nonfiction or writing scripts for computer games or interactive comic books?

The type of writing you like most and the companies that buy most of your articles, stories, or books will give you clues as to where you belong. Emerging Internet technology makes it possible to find the businesses that use the kind of writing you do best. As long as there's a wide enough audience to read what you write, there will be a market to sell the type of writing that most becomes you. Write for the needs of your audience and they will create your niche.

**Is print dead? No. Desktop Publishing is one of the fastest rising careers this decade. The same goes for computerized Graphic Design. See: http://www. nytimes.com/yr/mo/day/front/scan.html**

A scanned version of the front page of the *New York Times* can be displayed in both headline and digest form, with links to the articles. (Compare this front page to their interactive front page on page 6. It's the same issue—one in hypertext and the other in print.)

Recent changes in communication technology promise major overhauls in journalism and thus in journalism education. It may or may not be true that traditional media, especially print media, are doomed. But it certainly is true that those of us involved in journalism at all levels are challenged to adapt our traditional values and skills to new means of information delivery.

It's both frightening and gratifying to see journalists devoting significant effort to make their respecting media fit the newer forms. At first these changes will simply be add-ons to what we've done for years, but then we'll be challenged to find a synthesis that maintains many of the older values of journalism within the new electronic context. Some media are ahead of others, but it will be a slow process for most.

It's going to be especially necessary that professional journalists and journalism educators work together in full cooperation if we are to meet the challenge. We must help each other if, collectively, we are to continue to provide information in a form that is useful to the society we serve.

In journalism education, we are fighting to keep up and to move ahead. Our young people, the journalists of tomorrow, must be equipped for the communication revolution that we all see on the horizon. This is not simply a matter of helping students find jobs. It is more important that they understand the newer forms of communication technology because that technology will result in different methods of information retrieval and distribution.

Journalism schools must provide education, not simply training. Our students must be part of the change, not simply challenged by it. And we in education must move quickly to provide them with opportunities to understand both the technological and social implications of the journalism that will become dominant during their careers.

In the E.W. Scripps School of Journalism at Ohio University, we are working hard to find both the economic and human resources to create such opportunities for our students. We know that budgets will be stretched, and faculty members will be forced to learn new techniques.

We now offer several new classes and hope to modify our entire curriculum. Among classes added has been one that helps students gain usage of electronic data bases and other sources of information and one that is devoted specifically to Web pages and journalism. We will have other new classes, but it will be more important that we analyze our entire curriculum and find ways to integrate the newer forms, not simply add them to what we've done for years.

At the same time, it is crucial for journalism that we not pay too much attention to technology. Technology remains a means to an end. If our students are to succeed, they must fully appreciate how important journalistic values may be woven into newer forms of distribution. We must give our students the ability to distinguish themselves from the millions of others who will use the technology to communicate but will not understand or appreciate the distinction between true journalism and simple communication.

Bio

Ralph Izard is Director of the E.W. Scripps School of Journalism at Ohio University.

As an educator, author, and journalist, Izard has a broad range of experience with a special interest in issues related to ethics, the First Amendment, public affairs reporting, and news writing.

Voices from the industry:
Ralph Izard, Ph.D., Director, School of Journalism

The E. W. Scripps School of Journalism offers academic programs in Advertising Management, Broadcast News, Magazine and News Writing, Editing, and Public Relations. Their site includes a wealth of information, including hot links to online resources.

http://www.scripps.ohiou.edu

In a speech to a near capacity audience at UCSD on May 8, 1996, veteran journalist Daniel Schorr, 81, stated that the media and the public have split. "Journalism has been absorbed by a vast entertainment industry controlled from the corporate boardrooms of giant conglomerates."

If this is so, then will the Internet reunite them? When seasoned journalists downsized from dailies enter new careers, will it be as fiction writers of computer game scripts or as producers of digital and immersive video or interactive programming? Can three-dimensional writing skills be interchangeable with visionary writing and reporting the news?

Schorr said that the press has somehow lost its relationship with the American public, that the media is perceived as another anti-people institution, like government or business. Schorr explained, "No one looks at journalism anymore as a separate entity. It's now a part of something else."

If it has become a dangerous hybrid appearing in the form of such programs as daytime talk shows, then why are the ratings so high? When the hoards of television viewers invade the Internet, will it become the traffic-burdened Interknot—offering the same kind of immersive dumbed-down tabloid programming that is so popular on daytime TV?

It's up to the writer to determine what online journalism and interactive storytelling will become—writing from the bones or writing to make an impact on the emotions. Will writing that appeals to the heart find a larger audience than writing that appeals to the head, to logic and reason? Does propaganda as fiction sell well to the emotions? Yes! But, is that the world we want to build?

The fate of online journalism is up to the writer and producer as a team. What you get is what you write or design, and what sells is what the audience demands.

## Writing Drama or Memoirs as Time Capsules For Internet Theater Using Word Perfect Office Suite 12 (or later) and Corel Graphics Suite 12 (or later)?

Most freelance writers have not been exposed to fiction on Internet radio broadcasts. Yet writing for Internet theatre is a great way to put your life story on the Internet in the form of a radio play or narrated storytelling presentation.

Tool-centric writers meet the unwired majority of fiction writers, and what results? Multicast content is produced. In the recent past, writers of fiction who wanted to create and produce multicast content had to buy software such as Adobe Premiere, Ulead's Media Studio, Sonic Foundry's Sound Forge, and other tools such as SoftBook Maker, an output media that helps you put your project on a CD.

Now, with popular DVD that is quickly making VHS tapes obsolete, digital video disk, digital TV, and high definition TV, desktop publishers, graphic designers, and writers are looking for ways to distribute projects on disks or on the Internet. As fiction writers incorporate multimedia presentations for distance learning into their entertainment scripts and mixed-media of partial fiction and partial fact (as in demonstrating safety procedures in a training film using dramatic sequences), producing custom looks in multicast content is king. At the same time, fiction writers have to face learning curves.

At first, increasing numbers of job-hunting entertainment script writers and fiction authors ran to learn more about MPEG content. Multicasting meant learning how to stream MPEG files.

Decisions had to be made whether to use Wintel or Mac platforms, as if it mattered. It really depends on your goals as a fiction writer. Do you want to move into writing entertainment scripts for distance learning, music videos on the Internet, or dramatic writing for interactive books, games, or scripts? It has been said that you get to the universal through the concrete, and writers are looking for practical tips they can use right away.

Writers who dislike complicated computer manipulations to get to the content are asking multicast solution manufacturers to provide more push technology directly to PCs rather than require the writer/producer teams to worry about emerging compressors. Writing fiction for multicast is a collaborative process between a content writer working with creative problem solving in the fiction genres and producers who must learn to implement file formats and more choices between compressors and which platforms to use.

A producer's world is focused on deciding on which codecs are best suited for multicasting. A writer's world consists of contacting the manufacturers such as Precept, Apple, and Microsoft to find out what standards based on what works best works for them in the fiction/entertainment/education marketplace. Distance learning is being combined in new ways with music TV and entertainment scriptwriting to dramatize training video scenes.

Writers await maturity in multicasting tools, and producers seek maturity of imagination in writers in their ability to think child-like to attract new markets of wider age ranges. As producers go about setting the audio attributes in a desktop video capture session, writers work at editing the movie from inside the script to make it work right on the Internet. Producers capture the image. Authors capture the audience.

What a screenwriter on the Internet wants is to capture a raw movie and store, edit, and compress it for PC use. A writer's goal is to take a certain package to a producer. That package would contain an H.261 clip, for example, suitable for multicasting on a local area network (LAN). In addition, the clip would be used in what scriptwriters call internetworking environments. What would a scriptwriter need besides a fast computer?

What the fiction writer needs most is the ability and skill to do serious desktop editing. You have a choice of collaborating with a producer or learning production skills yourself by boning up on your knowledge of multicasting editing procedures. I highly recommend a book such as Web Developer's Guide to Multicasting, by Nels Johnson, Coriolis Group Books, 1997.

It will give a writer basic skills in producing for PCs. Before you choose a producer with which you'd collaborate, at least you would have the choice of producing yourself if you wanted to, and you'd learn new multicasting skills that come in handy when you are writing video scripts for PC or Internet broadcast, regardless of whether you write fiction, faction, docudrama, or fact. Software is out there for video editing, such as Adobe Premiere for Windows or Ulead Systems' Media Studio Pro, and others. So whether you use a MAC or an IBM-compatible computer, you are looking for a way to get your raw movie into your software project.

Streaming audio must be dramatic to capture the audience for the short attention span they'll spend on the screen—four minutes, without drifting away. Producers use software such as Sound Forge, or to test for short spans, Windows Sound Recorder, which allows you to save WAV files in certain formats. It's like a new world for scriptwriters to study multicasting production skills and get their fingers in the MPEG-1 content world where desktop video is captured in MPEG files on a PC working with video tape.

Fiction writers in all genres are now looking into software such as Adobe Photoshop, MoviePlayer, and ConvertToMovie software. These programs are movie playing and editing applications if you use QuickTime for the Mac. Or you can use Macromedia's SoundEdit, an audio file editor that's similar to Windows application Sound Forge.

The point is whether you learn multicasting skills or not, cross-platform skills are increasingly in demand for writers seeking work. Cross-platform production software helps producers convert from one type of software to another. Cross-platform skills enable a fiction writer to help on the production team or wear the producer's hat when necessary, especially if budgets are tight. If you're a writer who wants to write for the multicasting industry, for multicasting on the Internet, or for push technology to PCs, you need to find the audience and use the software that works best to bring forth your script into entertainment or education.

Any writer who can capture and edit desktop video, especially desktop digital video headed for push technology PC markets and in-office audiences as well as entertainment users, needs to know about video and audio capture, multicasting production tools, and software that compresses video to multicast format.

Writers need to know what MPEG is all about. Emerging streaming codecs based on MPEG technology continue to help desktop videographers who must tune software with hardware to produce an MPEG movie on a PC. Writing scripts for computers frequently requires the writer to be a desktop producer able to multicast native MPEG files with software such as Precept's IP/TV. Fiction writers have to upgrade. Whether it's their skills they upgrade in basic good storytelling or their cross-platform skills on Windows or Mac, creative people accommodate the requirements of the multicast industry.

A new wave of work in multicasting is opening for content writers and script writers. What you need to enter the open door are the skills to use better applications of software. It's not only your writing skills wanted by producers. They want a team-mate that can handle the production side when asked to pitch in as well as write the PC content. New media production requires a lot of content writing, imagination, and great storytelling, but it also requires new skills of writers. You're not only a fiction writer anymore.

You're a multicaster. Your key to collaborating and cooperating with the competition is to learn cross-platform skills. Writing and production techniques as part of your continuing education for life-long learning in multicasting opens the door to a career in live multicasting, running a production studio, and writing the fiction. To capture the audience, you first have to learn to capture the video for PCs. In a world where writers run their IP/TV servers with a VCR, receive VCR streams with IP/TV viewers, and write stories for push technology that end up in PCs, you need more than imagination.

You need mobility. Why scratch the surface by only having fiction writing skills, when you can grab the big ticket? The way up for a fiction writer is to create best-selling novels or expand intranet management solutions that include new ways to use fiction to dramatize corporate training.

MPEG delivers video without compromise, so it has been said. Now, you as the writer, must deliver content that creates enterprise-wide video.

Digital video writers are hired to solve creative problems. Platforms such as IP/TV are used in employee communications, where a boss talks to workers and human resource departments train employees in either technical job skills, safety, or about how to fit in with the group and get along with difficult people under stress at work.

I highly recommend Corel's training programs, either online or in groups. Group training of any type of software use for any company or school makes use of a lot of multicasting using IP/TV. Distance learning trains by broadcasting courses from one location to students anywhere in the world. TV is also multicast or broadcast to desktop PCs. Multicast may be commercial or internal.

A writer could learn a lot by studying how MPEG delivers video, how it's integrated into other software, such as ActiveMovie, and how a writer can reach different types of audiences using fiction in new ways for human resources departments, distance learning, or employee training in dramatic new ways to train and show examples through dramatization, as in safety training videos. Your stories can sing on PCs in office rooms as well in living rooms seeking entertainment and escape, or courses that combine entertainment with learning to hold attention.

To write fiction for distance learning, you can create anything from courses on how to write fiction or produce it, to using a virtual drama script to teach a course in almost any subject from history of science to costume design for theater. Or you can teach great storytelling skills from around the world. A fiction writer's imagination is a proving ground for what good storytelling is all about in the world of multicast technology. Great storytelling is presentation aesthetics.

Fiction genres and imaginative scriptwriting may combine autobiography or biography with fiction, or be true stories written as if they were fiction (faction), or combine fact with fiction in a novel or script to dramatize a point. If you're a fiction writer seeking a job in a multicasting facility, you need multicasting skills. If you work at home as a novelist in any genre or switch and combine genres, seeking new directions is the only way out of a shrinking market for romance novels that don't make the midlist.

A writer looks at multicasting from several directions—analog video, digital video, multimedia, print, storytelling, verbal acrobatics, mood enhancement, audience participation, and audience identification. In your story, the best way to inspire your imagination to plotting is to select a proverb based on a long-line of experience, and see how it is condensed into the shortest possible storyline that connotes the experience.

It will teach you a lot about condensing and compression of story plot into the briefest number of words that actually tells the story without rambling or excess words. Keep your sentences to ten words, but vary shorter sentences with longer ones in places to prevent monotony and flat writing.

Make your practical tips within a fiction story as interesting as the proverb you use. Let the value of real-world experience come through even the most fantasy-based stories that occur in other galaxies. Real-world experience is valuable in fiction. Be a mentor and work to create communities of mentors among the fiction writing, reading, producing, marketing, and publishing communities.

New people learn from working writers, and writers learn from producers the business side of multicasting fiction online. Talk to distance education producers who are interested in development. Distance learning is an exploding market for writers. There's room for fiction in the dramatizations that show how people act in a variety of situations. Build industry relationships between the entertainment world of imaginative writing and the practical uses of fiction in training, theme parks, escape, games, interactive books, virtual theater, and entertainment.

I highly recommend learning desktop publishing and graphic design before you open your business as a writer, publisher, personal historian, genealogist, or publicist. Corel has one of the best training programs in the country. Take advantage of the opportunity to learn as much as you can about various types of software.

Become a software case history manager or success story manager as an independent contractor. Be aware of how much can be done with and learned from software if you're going to do scrap booking, keepsake album crafting, quilting design online, personal history, genealogy, anthropojournalism, desktop publishing, Web or graphic design, and marketing communications.

There's a whole new world out there in digital journalism and related information industry opportunities to express your creativity while filling a niche market for packaged information, intelligence, dissemination, sales, public relations, training and marketing communications. Take it from a retired online teacher. Writing and training online is a world class education.

## CONCLUSIONS

From Scrap Books to DNA-Driven Genealogy Time Capsules and Personal History Reports Generated With Desktop Publishing and Graphic Design Software.

If you decide to open an online, home-based DNA-driven genealogy reporting and production service, reports and time capsules could include the possible geographic location where the DNA sequences originated. Customers usually want to see the name of an actual town, even though towns didn't exist 10,000 years ago when the sequences might have arisen.

The whole genome is not tested, only the few ancestral markers, usually 500 base pairs of genes. Testing DNA for ancestry does not have anything to do with testing genes for health risks because only certain genes are tested—genes related to ancestry. And all the testing is done at a laboratory, not at your online business.

If you're interested in a career in genetics counseling and wish to pursue a graduate degree in genetics counseling, that's another career route. For information, contact The American Board of Genetic Counseling. Sometimes social workers with some coursework in biology take a graduate degree in genetic counseling since it combines counseling skills with training in genetics and in interpreting genetics tests for your clients.

How to Be a Personal Historian or Documentarian and Make Time Capsules: 5-Week Course

Also for Reference: DNA-Testing for Ancestry Company

Family Tree DNA (click on link)

1. Family Tree DNA—Genealogy by Genetics, Ltd.
World Headquarters
1919 North Loop West, Suite 110 Houston, Texas 77008, USA
Phone: (713) 868-1438 | Fax: (832) 201-7147

# More Information and Resources

Check out Instructional Videos and Audios at:
http://www.newswriting.net/writingvideos.htm
Also see articles and excerpts of books at: www.newswriting.net

List of Published Paperback Books in Print Written by Anne Hart

1. Title: How to Interpret Family History and Ancestry DNA Test Results for Beginners: The Geography and History of Your Relatives

ISBN: 0-595-31684-0

2. Title: Cover Letters, Follow-Ups, and Book Proposals: Samples with Templates

ISBN: 0-595-31663-8

3. Title: Writer's Guide to Book Proposals: Templates, Query Letters, & Free Media Publicity

ISBN: 0-595-31673-5

4. Title: Title: Search Your Middle Eastern & European Genealogy: In the Former Ottoman Empire's Records and Online

ISBN:0-595-31811-8

5. Title: Is Radical Liberalism or Extreme Conservatism a Character Disorder, Mental Disease, or Publicity Campaign?—A Novel of Intrigue—

ISBN: 0-595-31751-0

6. How to Write Plays, Monologues, and Skits from Life Stories, Social Issues, and Current Events—for all Ages.

ISBN: 0-595-31866-5

7. Title: How to Make Money Organizing Information

ISBN: 0-595-23695-2

8. Title: How To Stop Elderly Abuse: A Prevention Guidebook

ISBN: 0-595-23550-6

9. Title: How to Make Money Teaching Online With Your Camcorder and PC: 25 Practical and Creative How-To Start-Ups To Teach Online

ISBN: 0-595-22123-8

10. Title: A Private Eye Called Mama Africa: What's an Egyptian Jewish Female Psycho-Sleuth Doing Fighting Hate Crimes in California?

ISBN: 0-595-18940-7

11. Title: The Freelance Writer's E-Publishing Guidebook: 25+ E-Publishing Home-based Online Writing Businesses to Start for Freelancers

ISBN: 0-595-18952-0

12. Title: The Courage to Be Jewish and the Wife of an Arab Sheik: What's a Jewish Girl from Brooklyn Doing Living as a Bedouin?

ISBN: 0-595-18790-0

13. Title: The Year My Whole Country Turned Jewish: A Time-Travel Adventure Novel in Medieval Khazaria

ISBN: 0-75967-251-2

14. Winning Resumes for Computer Personnel, Barron's Educational Series, Inc.

ISBN: 0-7641-0130-7

15. Title: The Day My Whole Country Turned Jewish: The Silk Road Kids

ISBN: 0-7596-6380-7

16. Title: Four Astronauts and a Kitten: A Mother and Daughter Astronaut Team, the Teen Twin Sons, and Patches, the Kitten: The Intergalactic Friendship Club

ISBN: 0-595-19202-5

17. Title: The Writer's Bible: Digital and Print Media: Skills, Promotion, and Marketing for Novelists, Playwrights, and Script Writers. Writing Entertainment Content for the New and Print Media.

ISBN: 0-595-19305-6

18. Title: New Afghanistan's TV Anchorwoman: A novel of mystery set in the New Afghanistan

ISBN: 0-595-21557-2

19. Title: Tools for Mystery Writers: Writing Suspense Using Hidden Personality Traits

ISBN: 0-595-21747-8

20. Title: The Khazars Will Rise Again!: Mystery Tales of the Khazars
ISBN: 0-595-21830-X

21. Title: Murder in the Women's Studies Department: A Professor Sleuth Novel of Mystery
ISBN: 0-595-21859-8

22. Title: Make Money With Your Camcorder and PC: 25+ Businesses: Make Money With Your Camcorder and Your Personal Computer by Linking Them.
ISBN: 0-595-21864-4

23. Title: Writing What People Buy: 101+ Projects That Get Results
ISBN: 0-595-21936-5

24. Title: Anne Joan Levine, Private Eye: Internal adventure through first-person mystery writer?s diary novels
ISBN: 0-595-21860-1

25. Title: Verbal Intercourse: A Darkly Humorous Novel of Interpersonal Couples and Family Communication
ISBN: 0-595-21946-2

26. Title: The Date Who Unleashed Hell: If You Love Me, Why Do You Humiliate Me?
"The Date" Mystery Fiction Series
ISBN: 0-595-21982-9

27. Title: Cleopatra's Daughter: Global Intercourse
ISBN: 0-595-22021-5

28. Title: Cyber Snoop Nation: The Adventures Of Littanie Webster, Sixteen-Year-Old Genius Private Eye On Internet Radio
ISBN: 0-595-22033-9

29. Title: Counseling Anarchists: We All Marry Our Mirrors—Someone Who Reflects How We Feel About Ourselves. Folding Inside Ourselves: A Novel of Mystery
ISBN: 0-595-22054-1

30. Title: Sacramento Latina: When the One Universal We Have In Common Divides Us
ISBN: 0-595-22061-4

31. Title: Astronauts and Their Cats: At night, the space station is cat-shadow dark

ISBN: 0-595-22330-3

32. Title: How Two Yellow Labs Saved the Space Program: When Smart Dogs Shape Shift in Space

ISBN: 0-595-23181-0

33. Title: The DNA Detectives: Working Against Time

ISBN: 0-595-25339-3

34. Title: How to Interpret Your DNA Test Results For Family History & Ancestry: Scientists Speak Out on Genealogy Joining Genetics

ISBN: 0-595-26334-8

35. Title: Roman Justice: SPQR: Too Roman To Handle

ISBN: 0-595-27282-7

36. Title: How to Make Money Selling Facts: to Non-Traditional Markets

ISBN: 0-595-27842-6

37. Title: Tracing Your Jewish DNA For Family History & Ancestry: Merging a Mosaic of Communities

ISBN: 0-595-28127-3

38. Title: The Beginner's Guide to Interpreting Ethnic DNA Origins for Family History: How Ashkenazi, Sephardi, Mizrahi & Europeans Are Related to Everyone Else

ISBN: 0-595-28306-3

39. Title: Nutritional Genomics—A Consumer's Guide to How Your Genes and Ancestry Respond to Food: Tailoring What You Eat to Your DNA

ISBN: 0-595-29067-1

40. Title: How to Safely Tailor Your Food, Medicines, & Cosmetics to Your Genes: A Consumer's Guide to Genetic Testing Kits from Ancestry to Nourishment

ISBN: 0-595-29403-0

41. Title: One Day Some Schlemiel Will Marry Me, Pay the Bills, and Hug Me.: Parents & Children Kvetch on Arab & Jewish Intermarriage

ISBN: 0-595-29826-5

42. Title: Find Your Personal Adam And Eve: Make DNA-Driven Genealogy Time Capsules

ISBN: 0-595-30633-0

43. Title: Creative Genealogy Projects: Writing Salable Life Stories

ISBN: 0-595-31305-1

44. Title: Power Dating Games: What's Important to Know About the Person You'll Marry

ISBN: 0-595-19186-X

45. Title: Problem-Solving & Cat Tales for the Holidays—Historical—Time Travel—Adventure. ISBN: 0-595-32692-7, Published September 2004.